KID KAPERS

USING SCIENCE FOR LEARNING LANGUAGE

JUDITH BULMER M.A.

SCIENCE AND LANGUAGE PRESS
LAKEWOOD, COLORADO

Copyright © 1995 by Judith Bulmer

Published by:

Science and Language Press
P.O. Box 150809
Lakewood, CO 80215

Publisher's Cataloging in Publication Data
(Prepared by Quality Books, Inc.)

Bulmer, Judith
    Kid kapers : using science for learning language / Judith
Bulmer.
    p. cm.
    Includes bibliographical references.
    ISBN 0-9642403-0-0

    1. Language arts (Elementary)--United States. 2. Science--Study
and teaching (Elementary)--United States. I. Title.

LB1576.B85 1994   372.6
                                    QBI94-1511

LCCN: 94-067964

ISBN: 0-9642403-0-0

Printed in the United States of America.

This book is dedicated to those who had the most influence on my life - my parents and sister, my husband, Ashley; and my children, Joseph and Jennifer.

TABLE OF CONTENTS

ACKNOWLEDGMENTS

Many gracious people supported me during the writing of this book. I want to thank Kathy Balog, Diana Rhody, Sharon Richards, Cathy Russell, La Vonna Sailor, and Keek Schiavone for their support and encouragement, Ann Hamilton for her enthusiasm and confidence, Janelle Britenstein for her wonderful suggestions, and Debbie, Morgan and Ryan Healy for having fun with the experiments. I am grateful to you all.

The publisher and the author have made every reasonable effort to ensure that the experiments and activities in this book are safe when carried out as instructed. They assume no responsibility or liability for any damage caused or sustained while conducting any of the experiments or activities. Parents, guardians, and/or teachers should supervise young children who undertake the experiments and activities in this book.

INTRODUCTION

The children are in the kitchen with mother when they return from shopping and the grocery store. As they put the groceries away, mom asks, "Do you think we could put water in these paper grocery bags?" She waits for the kids to answer, then asks, "Will the paper bag your new clothes came in or your lunch bag hold water?" "Let's find out!"

Kid Kapers was written for parents, grandparents, teachers and caretakers of children, preschool through second grade. The purpose is to provide a technique for adults to strengthen children's language experiences using science.

Superior language skills improve your child's ability to express and clarify his ideas, expand intellectual capacity, and help children gain control over reading, mathematics, and oral and written language. This gives them control over achievement in school and future success.

Research has shown that a helpful parent plays a crucial role in a child's school performance. They are their child's first teachers and are the everyday adult role models for language and thinking. For that reason, parents play the most influential role in their child's education and development.

These activities and experiments will help you create a language rich environment that will assist children in developing their powers of inner speech and their capacities to think, learn, plan, solve problems, understand, and manipulate language and the signs and symbols we use for reading, writing, communication, mathematics and science.

The beginning of the book discusses how children learn, the learning environment, and the importance of language.

Each experiment lists the equipment needed, the procedure to follow when doing the experiments, the expected results, and why the results occurred.

At the end of each experiment is a children's book or poetry that relates to the experiment in some way. The relationship may be in the title, the content of the book, the science activity, or an ecological implication from the experiment. The books are included because enjoyment of reading has been proven to increase language skills.

Before doing the experiments, read them carefully. Gather the needed supplies. During the experiments, use the suggestions for learning language and ask many questions. Observe the experiments and compare the results with those in the book. If your results are not the same as what is described in the book, be a scientist, problem solve, and start the experiment over again.

It is hoped that the adults involved will extend and elaborate on the activities to best meet their particular needs. But most of all, it is hoped that you will enjoy the time with your children as they discover the world about them. Be a curious scientist and have fun!

Judith Bulmer
Lakewood, Colorado
August, 1994

LANGUAGE DEVELOPMENT

The power to think is dependent upon language development because thinking is accomplished by using inner language. Using inner language for internalizing experiences helps organize thinking and makes the connection between action and thought and thought and action. Consequently, language development is the basis of the growth of the mind.

Language is a two-way process. There needs to be a balance between receiving and understanding language (hearing and processing), and expressing linguistic messages (speaking and communicating). We hear and process when we listen and read. We express when we talk and write. This is one of the first concepts children need to comprehend. Children need to be able to focus on and attend to whatever or whoever is giving input. Listening and understanding form the organizational basis of language and must come before expressive language. Children must understand language before they can generate it for communication, reading and writing.

Receptive and expressive language processing is based on the completion of a succession of learned skills. Young children begin language processing by gathering information and attaching meaning to the information. The next step is storing the information in an organized manner. Finally, children need to be able to retrieve the stored information for use whenever it is needed. These basic processing abilities are the prerequisites for the higher abilities of awareness of auditory information and language conceptualization. Language conceptualization is knowing and understanding what the content of language is, knowing and understanding the structure and rules of language, the ability to maintain the topic when having a conversation, and the ability to speak appropriately to a variety of listeners.

As the preschool to first grade years progress, children increase their use of language because it accompanies their play and learning. They begin to understand that everything has structure and they use language to internalize this structure. They expand their knowledge of the elements they have used to construct learning strategies by using classification, seriation, numeration, reversibility, and coordination.

Classification, the ability to sort items into pre-established categories, exists at many levels. For a child it may be sorting the silverware and for an adult it could be sorting receipts to do the income tax.

Seriation is organizing material into a sequential order. Young children may arrange toys from smallest to largest, school age children might decide what supplies they need to get before they start their homework, and mom decides what to cook first so that everything arrives at the table at the same time.

Numeration is the ability to manipulate numbers logically in solving mathematical problems ranging from how many popsicles to get for your friends to balancing the checkbook.

Reversability is knowing that something that can be done can also be undone.

Coordination is the ability to combine elements to make a set. I like apples and oranges is a linguistic example of coordination.

By building these learning strategies, students use language to accomplish their specific purposes. They become skillful at making language serve them to ask questions, answer questions, argue, greet and joke. When they can use language orally, they will be able to transfer these skills to writing.

Children ages four to six or seven are learning linguistic concepts that will help them function in the world. It is especially important that children have some knowledge of these concepts in order to function in school. Instructions for moving about, reading, mathematics, and doing class work involve these concepts. Important concepts include same, different, whole, part, behind, in front, first, last, middle, between, next to, beside, several, as many as, other, farthest, nearest, alike, never, always, match, center, forward, backward, medium sized, half separated, skip, widest, narrowest, few and pair.

Children ages four to six or seven are also learning language to express themselves. Sentence length increases from four to seven words at four years old to seven to

4

twelve words at seven years old. Their language is also getting more complex. By the time they are six years old, children use correct verb tenses, can answer "what happens if" questions, can discuss attributes such as color, shape and size, can state similarities and differences between objects (compare and contrast), begin to describe cause and effect relationships, can describe location and movement of objects, name positions of objects, and use comparatives and superlatives (for example big, bigger, biggest).

Language increases brain functioning, develops mental skills that contribute to academic achievement, and is the foundation for math and scientific reasoning as well as reading and writing. Learning language using science will give children a distinct advantage when the emphasis in learning is changing from remembering to understanding, organizing and problem solving. Using science to learn language is a way of empowering children. There can be no greater gift!

ACTIVE LEARNING

Jean Piaget, one of the most respected and quoted scholars in the area of children's intellectual development, states that children construct intelligence as they manipulate objects and interact with individuals and with their environment. The development of the ability to think and learn in logical patterns comes through exploring. Children acquire knowledge from their own action on their surroundings, not from what we tell them. This is defined as active learning.

Active learning involves projects where children make associations between newly discovered ideas and their previous perceptions of how the world works. They create meaning for themselves by connecting previous structure and framework with new experiences and learning. They use their senses to obtain information through observation, helping to actively construct their interpretation of what the world is like.

Children learn through play. During play experiences the child learns problem solving skills, spatial relationships, sequencing, structural relationships, and logical thinking. They are also learning the math concepts of measurement, comparison, size and number, and the scientific concepts of gravity, force, motion, and cause and effect. Most importantly, as they learn all of these concepts, they learn the language necessary to go with them.

The experiments in this book represent the enormous opportunities for learning while doing science experiments. As children do these activities, they interact with objects in the world around them and they build their image of the world at their level of development and according to their experiences. As they move to higher stages of development, they reconstruct their ideas so that they become more objective. As children discover and learn about their world through active experiences, they reorganize their thinking, and consequently deal with more complicated information. When children learn new information, they change their thinking patterns to conform with their new insights and knowledge. Understanding a new experience grows out of what was learned during a preceding one. At each level of development, children comprehend new information based on what was understood during a previous level making development cumulative. It is through doing that children are able to modify and refine their concept formation and the language that goes with this learning. Children need repeated active learning experiences to make associations, generalize information, and increase language. Active learning is significant because:

- Thought comes from actions not from words.

- Active learning is discovering for oneself.

- Getting information is passive, experiencing information is active.

- Active learning allows the child to produce an effect on the world.

- Children construct their own knowledge through repeated experiences involving interaction with people and materials.

- Knowledge and language are constructed as a result of dynamic interactions between the individual and the physical and social environments.

- Children play an active role in the growth of their language as they learn by doing.

- Motivation and learning can be generated by hands-on experience-oriented activities.

Remember, children need to create their own explanations and keep trying them out through intellectual processes and physical manipulations. Experiencing the environment is the key! Participation is the name of the game!

THE LEARNING ENVIRONMENT

Young children can learn much more than we have been led to believe. Recent research has proven that given the opportunity, children easily understand and master information at a young age.

To learn successfully, children must become good listeners and the practice of listening can be taught. When working with younger children, it is important to begin by describing one task to do at a time. As children develop understanding and memory, more than one job can be explained. When you begin, give the instructions and check to be certain that they are understood. Help the children carry out the activities, if necessary. Remember that younger children do not always use the language connections that are obvious to you. Even if meaning seems clear in your context, do not assume it is equally clear to children.

Three important characteristics that influence learning situations are enjoyment, interest and success. As the adult working with children on these activities, you are able to influence the circumstances surrounding the learning environment. You will decide on the space and organize the area to be used. Provide a setting that allows children to explore. Design projects so the children can take care of things themselves. Help them find a container to put science experiment supplies in and have a special place to put it. Assist them in keeping a notebook or making a comic strip with writings and drawings about their experiences. These will enhance children's interest in the experiments and enjoyment of the activities which will increase success in reading and writing skills as well as language.

A great deal of the time you spend with your children may take place in the kitchen or outside. These are perfect locations for carrying out these projects and making your own science laboratory. Almost everything you need can be found in your home. In most cases, inexpensive household objects and materials are used.

One of the purposes of this book is for the children to function independently but with adult guidance and supervision. A few experiments require adult assistance and should not be done by children alone. These projects are clearly identified. Before starting the experiment check the text to be certain you have the necessary equipment and to know the vocabulary and language to emphasize for each activity.

It is important to let the children decide how to carry out the experiment and what the results mean to them. Adults can model and facilitate language and thinking when they are working directly with the children or while they are doing their jobs in the same location. Ask children "What do you think will happen?" This question will help them learn and understand cause and effect, prediction, comparison, and evaluation. Another question to ask is "What did you do?" Sequencing, classifying, observing, summarizing, seriation, interpreting, and evaluation will be addressed by this question. Remember, the purpose of the activities is to increase children's language and thinking using science. When adults and children work together, children observe the way adults accomplish tasks. They see the adult's perspective in careful planning, their patience in completing work and the serious thought that goes into evaluating their accomplishments. Children gain self esteem working beside an adult, especially when that grown-up can establish the child's feeling of self worth through facial expressions, gestures, words and actions.

Children need self confidence in order to be effective learners. You have heard many times that success breeds success. For that reason, you need to arrange experiences for your children in a way that allows much more success than failure. As children go from success to success with ideas and language, their potential for further development increases.

By working near or with your child, you will be able to encourage good social interaction which is the essence of communication. To learn language, children need to be surrounded with it. They need to be alert to the usefulness of words everywhere. Talk to your child as you do these projects. Use the suggestions for vocabulary and language at the beginning of each section. Use language familiar to the children you are working with. Ask probing questions

10

rather than giving answers and explanations. Show how concepts and word meanings work together to clarify the meaning of language that may be unfamiliar. Unfamiliar information must be talked about in order for it to become a part of children's understanding.

Encourage observation of objects and actions. Through careful observation, vocabulary increases and a groundwork is laid for verbal expression. Progress in building vocabulary and using conversation increases language ability and builds the potential for thinking. Research has shown that when parents talk to their children and react to what they say, not how they say it, children learn language more quickly and better, and are more likely to achieve rapidly in school.

From the beginning, children develop language and thinking skills by listening, watching and experiencing their environment. The senses become the gateway to the mind. Therefore, in order to learn in the best manner, children must demonstrate active exploration of their surroundings. An experience that allows children to physically explore objects helps them make sense of abstract ideas.

Attention must be on the process of learning rather than the product. Allow children to make mistakes and learn from them without telling them they are wrong. Remember that learning occurs during the process of reaching a solution, even if the solution itself isn't particularly satisfactory. Give children time to carry out their projects. When children need more time than is available, help them plan for another day when they can work on their project again. Helping children complete projects lets them know that what they're doing is important.

When planning activities, include choices. Help children examine them and choose the ones they want. Recognize their choices and decisions when they make them. Help children be aware that they've made a choice and of the control they have over their own actions. It is often helpful for children and adults to work together. Children need to ask questions and be allowed to react to questions. They need to talk about their ideas and solve problems together. This allows them to explain their thinking to others, to understand how others think and to structure rationale for problem situations. The conversations they have will help them clarify ideas and increase their ability to communicate. Help children

11

support and talk to each other by encouraging them to show others what they've accomplished.

Direct children's attention to projects, events, and associations worth describing. Encourage them to explain by answering their own questions (What do you have? What do you think it is?). Provide opportunities for children to describe what they're going to do (Plan), describe what they are doing (Do), and describe what happened (Review).

Planning involves designing the process to use to do the experiments. Encourage children to use language to describe what to do and how to go about it. When children communicate about the process it helps them form a mental picture of their ideas so they know where to start and how to proceed. Some questions to ask are:

- What do we need to do this experiment?

- When is the best time to do it?

- Where is the best place to do it?

- Who will work with you?

- What will you do first? . . . last?

Children who plan, see that they can make things happen and that they can act on their decisions. For adults, discussing a plan provides an opportunity to encourage and respond to children's ideas.

Doing involves locating and arranging materials, carrying out the experiments in logical order, discovering problems, and exploring and evaluating solutions to problems. This is the time to use the most questions and discussion. Some questions to ask are:

- What do you need next?

- Tell me how you did that?

- How do you know that's right?

- What would happen if . . . ?

- What do you think the problem is?

Review can be done during clean-up time. Recall and discuss what was done during planning for the experiment and how the experiment was carried out. This helps children see the relationships between their plans and their activities. In the process of remembering what they have done, children attach language to their actions. This helps them build on what they've learned and remember it when they plan for the next experiment. Some questions and comments for reviewing are:

- What do you think was the best part?

- Put the steps of the experiments in order.

- Retell what happened in the experiment.

- Compare what you thought would happen with what really happened.

Discuss the processes used and the results of the projects with the children and encourage them to think of explanations for why the project happened the way it did.

Children learning language using science have confidence in themselves and their abilities. With confidence children succeed in doing tasks far beyond our expectations.

Source: *Young Children in Action.* Mary Hohmann, Bernard Banet and David P. Weikart. High Scope Press, Michigan, 1979.

INTELLIGENT COMMUNICATION

Language is learned by hearing and using purposeful and meaningful communication in an encouraging and supportive environment. Communication with children should acknowledge and describe what they are doing and should reinforce and support the children so they experience success. Children should be given time and opportunity to respond and contribute.

Adults serve as a guide and encourage children's spontaneous development. This means that they create situations in which children work and learn by themselves for themselves. They create an environment where children feel safe to express their thinking, where there is mutual trust between adults and children, and where there is a difference between criticizing ideas and criticizing people. Since your major role is a facilitator for discovery rather than a dispenser of knowledge, you assist children to make the connections necessary to associate the science activities with language.

Establish an atmosphere where all communication, exchanges of information, and answers are acceptable. Keep away from an environment where responses are judged as right or wrong. Keep children actively involved, don't let them sit and watch. Talk your way through the activities and experiments because out loud communication benefits all of the areas of language. Verbalizing what you and the children are thinking and feeling will help them to acquire vocabulary and language and be actively involved.

Use vocabulary familiar to the children. When they can connect new words to those they already know, there is greater likelihood the new vocabulary will be remembered. The same is true for language and sentence forms as well as experiences. Children who can see how new experiences relate to old ones have more organized strategies for communicating the information they know. Ask a lot of questions while you work. Different questions require different kinds of thinking so analyze the type of thinking

15

you are after before asking the questions. The questions do not always need to be answered because science is a process of inquiry.

When children ask you questions, do not give immediate answers but use their questions as a starting point for exploring ideas. To be asked questions and to react to questions builds a foundation for language and solving problems. Adults need to involve children in conversation using probing questions that require children to investigate, organize, justify, explain and reconsider their original reaction and responses in light of more information. Monitor children's comprehension of statements and questions and rephrase them if necessary. Pay special attention to the responses children give and why those responses were made. This will provide knowledge on how to phrase questions to get the most information in reply.

Use an open-ended questioning approach that gives children opportunities to reflect on their thinking and work. Prevent children from answering impulsively. Slow down the answering process so that real thinking can occur. Have children repeat the question silently to themselves while they visualize the kind of answer the question is looking for. Then, guide them to get their ideas into words. Use vocabulary that will start them thinking. Examples of thinking words are: label, group, find, show, change, choose, organize, search, sort, create, predict, determine and evaluate. The pages at the end of this section will give you more ideas. Remember, the goal when doing the science experiments and projects in this book is to give children strategies to be competent and successful when sharing information.

Research shows that children who can speak thoughtfully and reflectively about problems and strategies to solve them are better communicators, readers, writers and thinkers. Delight in the benefits of these projects - they show the way for children to communicate and express themselves in a powerful and successful manner.

PROCESS QUESTIONS

How To Ask Questions About The Process Of Doing

- What do you need to do next?

- Tell me how you did that?

- What do you think would happen if . . . .?

- When have you done something like this before?

- How would you feel if . . . .?

- Yes, that's right, but how do you know it is right?

- When is another time you need to . . . .?

- What do you think the problem is?

- Can you think of another way we could do this?

- Why is this one better than that one?

- How can you find out?

- How is . . . . different (like) . . . .?

Source: Carl Haywood, Vanderbilt University

QUESTIONS FOR MORE INFORMATION

Helpful Phrases For Increasing Communication

Recognizing Responses

- That's a new idea.

- You really thought about that one.

- I see.

- Interesting. That's an interesting point.

Reflecting Responses

- You're wondering if . . . .?

- You want to know . . . .?

- Does that mean . . . .?

- Are you saying . . . .?

- It sounds as if you're thinking (feeling) . . . .

- You think . . . .?

- You're disagreeing with . . . .?

Explaining Responses

- Why do you say that?

- Can you tell me more about . . . .?

- I don't understand what you mean.

- That's interesting, tell me more.

- What do you mean by that?

Contradictory Responses

- That's an idea I never heard before.

- That's an interesting idea; have you thought about .?

- You thought hard about that answer, but could it be that . .?

- Here's another thought . . . .

Challenging Responses

- I wonder how we know . . . .?

- If that's true, then is . . . . also true?

- Can you give some reasons for . . . .?

Redirecting Responses

- How does that relate to what was just said?

- Maybe we should talk about that idea next time. We still need to talk about . . . .

- Interesting idea, let's go back to . . . .

- That's a good point, but we haven't finished talking about .

Source: Is Your Bed Still There When You Close The Door? Jane M. Healy, Ph.D. Doubleday, New York, 1992.

WORDS TO USE TO INCREASE LANGUAGE
Preschool - Kindergarten

LEVELS OF LEARNING	WORDS TO START QUESTIONS
KNOWLEDGE Know facts, ideas and vocabulary. Remember.	Remember, Show, Tell, List, Match, Describe, Name, Repeat, Locate, Choose, Pick, Find, Group, Know.
COMPREHENSION Understand meaning of material, interpret and communicate learning.	Show, Find, Change, Retell, Describe, Give examples, Demonstrate.
APPLICATION Using what you know in a new situation. Solve problems.	Use, Solve, Collect, Act out, Put in order, Paint, Choose, Put together.
ANALYSIS Separating ideas into parts, seeing relationships, finding characteristics.	Examine, Arrange, Compare, Categorize, Sort, Classify, Take apart.
SYNTHESIS Reorganize parts to create new ideas or concepts.	Build, Improve, Make up, Imagine, Pretend, Suppose, Create, Invent, What if.
EVALUATION Judging the value of information, making decisions.	Decide, Choose, Prove, Determine order, Come to conclusions.

Based on "Bloom's Taxonomy of Educational Objectives"

WORDS TO USE TO INCREASE LANGUAGE Primary Level	
LEVELS OF LANGUAGE	**WORDS TO START QUESTIONS**
KNOWLEDGE Know facts, ideas, and vocabulary. Remember.	Who, What, When, Where, Repeat, Name, Match, Describe, Choose, Match, Remember, Know, Recognize, Write, Report, Label, Underline.
COMPREHENSION Understand meaning of material, interpret and communicate learning.	Explain, Review, Why, Reword, Find, Summarize, Describe, Change, Reorganize, Give the main idea, Illustrate.
APPLICATION Using what you know in a new situation, solving problems.	Show, Report, Draw, Collect, Practice, Demonstrate, Use, Model, Act out, Classify.
ANALYSIS Separating ideas into parts, seeing relationships, finding characteristics.	Investigate, Survey, Separate, Test, Solve, Chart, Discover, Compare and contrast, Show how things are alike and different.
SYNTHESIS Reorganizing parts to create new ideas and concepts.	Imagine, Produce, Plan, Predict, Organize, Construct, Design, Improve, Formulate, Compose.
EVALUATION Judging the value of information, making decisions.	Judge, Argue, Select/Choose, Decide, Prove, Rate, Measure, Recommend, Grade, Justify.

Based on "Bloom's Taxonomy of Educational Objectives"

STRATEGIES FOR ORGANIZING AND INTEGRATING INFORMATION

Questions to ask:

- What things were really interesting?

- What would you like to know more about?

- What was the "big idea" for this project?

- What were the most important steps in this project?

- What is the important thing about . . . .?

- What is one word that describes what happened?

- Why did you choose that word?

- Ask one question about something that puzzles you.

Statements to start thinking:

- . . . . is (are) like . . . . because

- For older children, give them a letter of the alphabet and they must think of a word with that letter to describe the project.

- Tell what you know, what you think you know, and what you want to know.

- Say five words that occur to you when you think of . . . .

- Name something you learned today.

- State the evidence to show why something happened in the experiment.

Activities:

- Draw a picture of before and after.

- Draw a chain of events - what happened first, next, last.

- Draw a circle of events - what happened first, second, third and fourth.

- Make a chart to compare and contrast experiments.

- Make a chart to show the causes and effects of the experiments.

- Make a comic strip of the activities in the experiment.

- Literature: The Important Book by Margaret Wise Brown

WHY USE SCIENCE TO LEARN LANGUAGE?

Children's capability to learn language can be increased in a great number of ways. For that to happen, children must be involved in personal experiences and activities that stimulate various kinds of thinking. This will produce an abundance of language with rich content and is the primary purpose for using science to learn language.

Scientists bring attitudes to their work that increase language production. Scientists are logical, curious, and enjoy finding out why surprising events happen. They use all their senses to observe and figure out what happens during experiments. They ask questions and gather information about the questions, form and test theories, and then report findings to others.

PROCESSES SCIENTISTS USE TO INCREASE LANGUAGE		
observing	identifying	recognizing relationships
measuring	contrasting	forming hypothesis
collecting	interpreting	experimenting
comparing	sequencing	inferring
classifying	predicting	drawing conclusions reporting and recording

Recent research tells us that children learn language from active involvement; children organize concepts from repeatedly performing activities with objects. Capturing children's curiosity may be the fundamental ingredient in increasing knowledge and language development. Children who are interested and actively involved in a project are able to organize their experiences and the language that goes with them. Science activities improve language learning and school readiness in young children; discovering with science creates a structure for converting experiences into language, and science activities furnish experiences for greater generalization of information and language learning.

Children learn in different ways and science is a multi-sensory approach involving hands-on manipulation of objects, visual and auditory understanding, and kinesthetic skills (the sensation of position and movement).

Learning language using science is a dynamic, ongoing activity that creates opportunities for meaningful work to solve complex problems. It enables children to "see the connections," which allows them to understand and remember what they learn.

These attributes of science challenge children to use a variety of investigative experiences to increase use of language in the world around them. They discover "finding out" is fun.

EXPLORING WITH WATER

Water is one of the most common products of nature and holds a unique fascination for adults and children. It covers seventy five percent of the earth's surface and makes up two thirds of your body. It is one of the most versatile substances for learning language using science and provides a multitude of experiences for scientists of all ages.

Water has weight and pressure. Water weighs about eight and one-third pounds per gallon. This causes pressure when it sits on top of something.

Water is buoyant. This means things can float in water. The amount of air inside things and their shape determine their ability to float.

Water is found in three forms: liquid, gas and solid. Water is constantly changing from the liquid state to the vapor state and back again. Most of the water we use comes from the rain and snow that falls from the sky. Rain collects in puddles, lakes, ponds, and streams. The heat of the sun turns the water into an invisible mist called water vapor. The water vapor rises into the sky. In the sky, the air is cold. Cold air makes the water vapor turn into drops of water. When water vapor changes back to liquid water, it is called condensation. The condensation then falls as either rain or snow, depending on the temperature.

Water is a liquid when it is fluid and free flowing. Water is a gas when it is heated to a high temperature (one hundred degrees Celsius or two hundred twelve degrees Fahrenheit) and goes into the air as vapor. When water drops below the freezing point (below zero degrees Celsius or thirty two degrees Fahrenheit) it becomes the solid form which is ice.

Water is made of hydrogen and oxygen. Two atoms of hydrogen combine with one atom of oxygen to make a molecule of water.

Before beginning to explore water, provide children with experiences where they can classify water into its three forms. This will help them become familiar with the ideas that will be covered in the activities.

Every activity will stimulate lots of questions that will generate a lot of language learning. It is important for children to know there is no wrong answer and every finding is acceptable and legitimate. Remember, there are no wrong results!

EVAPORATION

Evaporation is defined as the process of drying by removing moisture. Moisture in the air is called humidity and is one part of the water cycle. Large amounts of water are always evaporating into the air when the sun heats the earth's oceans, lakes and rivers. These experiments will show how the water gets into the air.

VOCABULARY

As you work with children doing the experiments you can use these words to talk about what you are doing and what is happening. Use the vocabulary words when talking about the experiments so children hear and become familiar with them. Help the children use the different expressions when they describe, discuss and problem solve during the activities. You can make the decision about which words are appropriate for the children you are working with, but keep in mind that everyone understands at a higher level than they can express.

VOCABULARY			
Words to use and define in this section are:			
fat	melt	below	shallow
top	bulge	narrow	measure
less	clear	vanish	surface
more	small	escape	outside
deep	empty	higher	pressure
flat	below	inside	increase
wide	large	almost	melt down
tall	vapor	dry up	disappear
sink	equal	skinny	temperature

LANGUAGE

Ask children to describe what they see and what they are doing. As you discuss what is happening continue to use the vocabulary words for this lesson so children learn how you use them. This is a good chance to use comparing words like deep -deeper, small -smaller, and large -larger. Encourage children to come up with their own words to tell about what they see happening. Don't forget -there are no wrong answers, just more opportunities to solve problems.

PARENT NOTES

These activities may take as long as a week to finish. Try to find a spot where you can keep the containers undisturbed. Have your child make a "Please Do Not Disturb" sign to put by the containers.

ACTIVITIES

- The Hump On The Jar

- Water That Vanishes

- Cooling The Air

- Disappearing Water Competition

- Water And The Wind

- How Does Water Get Into The Air?

- Disappearing Water Contest

EVAPORATION
The Hump on the Jar

Equipment
- 2 similar jars
- rubber from a large broken balloon
- rubber bands
- water

Procedure

Fill one jar with water until it is almost full. Leave the other jar empty. Leave them in a warm room for a few hours until the temperature in each jar is the same.

Cover both jars with stretched pieces of the balloon and hold the balloon on with the rubber bands. Leave the jars overnight. Check them in the morning. What do you see? Leave them alone and check again in the afternoon. What do you see? Is it different?

Results
The balloon covering the jar of water will have a little hump. This is showing that the water tried to escape into the air and evaporate.

Why?
The evaporating water wants to escape and move into the air. This causes an increase in pressure in the air in the jar which is enough to make the balloon swell.

Literature
How The Camel Got His Hump
by Rudyard Kipling

Water That Vanishes

Equipment

- tall, clear, wide-mouthed container
- marking pen or tape
- water

Procedure

This experiment could take a few days to complete. Fill the container about three-fourths full of water. Use the tape or marker to record the level of the water. Each day look at the container and record the level of the water with the marker or tape. After a few days, compare the water level with the level when you started.

Results

The water level is way below the line you made when the container was first filled.

Why?

You can't see what is happening, but you can see that the water is no longer in the container. The water is vanishing into the air. This process is called evaporation.

Literature

The Magic Schoolbus At The Waterworks by Joanna Cole

33

Cooling The Air

Equipment
- thermometer
- cotton
- rubber band
- eyedropper or straw
- water

Procedure

Put the thermometer where the wind will blow around it. After about a half hour, write down the temperature. Wet a small piece of cotton. Squeeze some of the water out so it is just damp. Put the cotton around the bulb of the thermometer. Leave it in the same place in the wind for the same amount of time. Check it and write down the temperature.

Results

The temperatures you recorded show that the thermometer with the wet cotton on it has a temperature several degrees lower than the thermometer without the cotton.

Literature

Where Does It Come From?
by Kathy Henderson

Why?

Heat is removed from the thermometer during the process of evaporation. The damp cotton causes more of the energy to be removed in the form of heat. Have your parents help you look up hygrometer in the encyclopedia. How does this experiment relate to the hygrometer?

Water Out Of The Air

Equipment
- empty can
- ice cubes
- food coloring
- water

Procedure

Take the label off the can. Fill it with ice cubes.
Add a little water and a few drops of food coloring.
Leave the can on the table for a few minutes.

Results

Drops of water are building on the outside of the can and are beginning to slide down the sides. We say the can is "sweating."

Why?

Are the water drops colored? If they are colored they are leaking from the can. Are they leaking from the can? Air particles slow down and move closer together when they get cold. When they move closer, they become liquid. The water vapor in the air near the can has been cooled by the ice, so it turns to fluid. That's why a cold glass of lemonade gets very wet on the outside on a humid day.

Literature
The Rain Puddle
by Adelaide Hall

Disappearing Water Competition

Equipment
- 2 identical dishes
- sunny window
- food coloring
- water

Procedure

Fill each dish with the same amount of water. Put a few drops of different colored food coloring in each. Put one dish in a sunny window and the other in a place that gets no sun. Leave them all day and check them in the evening. If you wish, you can leave them for a second day.

Results
The dish in the sun dries first.

Why?

The particles of water move into the air and evaporate faster when the water is warm. The heat from the sun makes the water warmer so the dish in the sun evaporates faster. Will the sun cause a puddle to dry up faster? Measure a puddle and keep a chart of how much it dries up each day. Do you think the temperature can change the amount of time it takes for it to dry? Can you predict how long it will take for a puddle to dry up?

Literature
In The Middle Of The Puddle
by Mike Thaler

Water And The Wind

Equipment

- clothesline (or tie a string between two chairs)
- piece of cardboard 4" long by 4" wide
- 2 wet handkerchiefs

Procedure

Hang the two handkerchiefs on the clothesline to dry. Fan one of them with the cardboard.

Results

The handkerchief that was fanned with the cardboard dried first.

Why?

The fanning does the same thing as blowing winds. It speeds up evaporation by removing the moist air and putting drier air near the handkerchief. When laundry is hung outside, will it dry faster if the wind is blowing? When you wash the chalkboard at school, will it dry faster if you blow on it?

Literature

Gilberto And The Wind
by Marie Hall Ets

How Does Water Get Into The Air?

Equipment
- jar without a lid
- jar with a lid
- marker or tape
- water

Procedure

Place the same amount of water in each jar. Cover one of them. Mark the water level on the outside of the jars with a marker or tape. Put them in a safe place over night. Check them in the morning. Leave them alone and check them again that night.

Results

There will be less water in the jar without the lid.

Why?

Tiny particles of water in the jar without the lid move fast enough to escape into the air. This will happen no matter what the temperature of the water or the air. The water turns into water vapor. Is this what happens to puddles after a rain? Is this how water gets back into the air after a rain? What happens after a snowfall?

Literature
Follow The Water From Brook To Ocean by Arthur Dorros

38

Disappearing Water Contest

Equipment
- large flat dish
- food coloring
- deep narrow jar without a lid
- water

Procedure

Put some water in the dish. Add a few drops of your choice of food coloring. Put an equal amount of water in the deep narrow jar. Add a few drops of a different color food coloring. Put both containers in a safe place overnight. Check them in the morning. Leave them and check them again that night. Which container will evaporate faster?

Results

There is less water in the flat dish and more water in the narrow jar.

Why?

The tiny particles of water can escape only from the top or surface of the water. Therefore, the water will evaporate faster in the flat dish because the surface is larger than the surface in the deep narrow jar. Will a large shallow puddle dry up faster than a deep small one?

Literature

Bringing The Rain To Kapiti
by Verna Aardema

ENRICHMENT ACTIVITIES

The Misty Mirror

Have you noticed the steam on the mirror in the bathroom when you take a shower or a hot bath? The hot water from the shower or bath makes the air warm. Warm air holds more water than colder air and forms a coating on the mirror. How do you get the coating off the mirror? Will it go away faster if you open the door or if you leave the door closed? What if you blow the hot air from the hair dryer on the mirror? What if you blow cold air from the hair dryer on the mirror? When the mist on the mirror disappears, it evaporates.

Walls Covered With Water

Have you noticed the water drops that form on the wall of the bathroom when you take a shower or a hot bath? The warm air is holding more water, and when the warm air full of water meets the cold air on the walls, the temperature of the air is lowered. This is what makes the water drops on the walls. It is called condensation. Do you wipe the water off the walls? Does it just disappear? How long does it take? Does it take longer when the temperature is hot or cold? Can you use the hair dryer for this too? When the water drops disappear, they evaporate.

You're All Wet

How does your body feel when you get out of a hot bath or shower? The air feels cold until you get dry. When water is evaporating it uses energy. The energy it takes is in the form of body heat so you feel cold. What are some things you can do to keep from feeling cold when you get out of the shower or bath?

Salty Water

Remember all those experiments with two bowls of water? Can you predict what will happen if you have two bowls of water with equal amounts of water but one of them has some salt in it? What will happen when the water evaporates? Try it and discover the results.

40

SURFACE TENSION

One of the characteristics of water is surface tension. This means water has the ability to stick to itself and pull itself together. Water appears to be covered with a thin elastic-like coating. This coating is what makes it form drops instead of other shapes. Surface tension also allows water to be displaced by a floating object.

VOCABULARY

Some of these words are difficult to understand. Explain the vocabulary that pertains to each experiment as you do the experiment. Children will understand at different levels depending on their age.

VOCABULARY			
Words to use and define in this section are:			
mix	across	center	tightly
top	weaken	highest	farther
sink	slowly	surface	several
spurt	absorb	tension	separate
bulge	expand	combine	dissolve
spout	curved	compare	identical
float	bottom	forward	strengthen
cling			

LANGUAGE

Ask children to describe the equipment and make suggestions about how to use each item for the experiment. Encourage them to predict what they think will happen when they carry out the activity. When the activity is finished, have them compare their predictions with what actually happened. This is an opportunity for the adult to describe a change in the experiment and ask "what would happen if" questions. These activities lend themselves well to questions about cause and effect relationships, comparing and contrasting discussions, and communication about the properties of liquids.

PARENT NOTES

Before each experiment, review the concept of surface tension and the idea that the skin-like coating of the water will support the weight of a lightweight item. Explain to the children that scientists often do experiments many times to make just a small discovery.

ACTIVITIES

- Water Spout

- Colored Water Drops

- Sinking Water

- Soap Propelled Boat

- Side or Center

- Spurting Water

- Stringing Water Along

- Powdery Pursuit

SURFACE TENSION
Water Spout

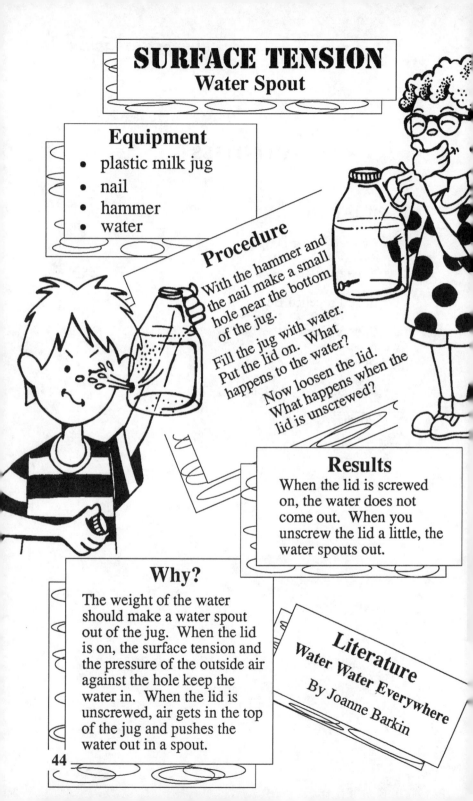

Equipment
- plastic milk jug
- nail
- hammer
- water

Procedure
With the hammer and the nail make a small hole near the bottom of the jug.

Fill the jug with water. Put the lid on. What happens to the water?

Now loosen the lid. What happens when the lid is unscrewed?

Results
When the lid is screwed on, the water does not come out. When you unscrew the lid a little, the water spouts out.

Why?
The weight of the water should make a water spout out of the jug. When the lid is on, the surface tension and the pressure of the outside air against the hole keep the water in. When the lid is unscrewed, air gets in the top of the jug and pushes the water out in a spout.

Literature
Water Water Everywhere
By Joanne Barkin

44

Colored Water Drops

Equipment
- yellow and blue food coloring
- drinking glasses, jars or cups
- plastic drinking straws • water
- freezer wrap • dish soap
- paper towels

Procedure

Mix yellow food coloring and water in one of the jars. Mix blue food coloring and water in a second jar. Give each child a piece of freezer wrap, a straw, and some yellow water. Put the straw in the yellow water, fold about an inch at the top down, and put drops of water on the freezer wrap. Experiment with different ways of moving the drops around on the paper. What happens when the drops touch one another? Can you make one big drop? Can you separate the big drops into smaller ones? What are the different ways to move the drops? Do the same thing with the blue drops. What happens when the blue and yellow drops touch each other?

Results

When the drops get near one another they seem to come together and make bigger drops. You can also use the straw to make big drops into little ones. You can move the drops in many ways including blowing and using the straws. When the yellow drops and blue drops mix they become green.

Why?

The water drops move together because water molecules have a strong attraction for each other. Yellow and blue become green because they are primary colors.

Literature

Mouse Paint
by Ellen Stoll Walsh

45

Expanding Water

Equipment

- clear plastic drinking glass • water
- pitcher or cup with a spout
- eyedropper   • paper towels
- 100 metal paper clips
- 100 pennies

Procedure

Do not let the glass overflow during this experiment. If this happens, start over. Put the glass in the middle of the paper towel. Use the pitcher to fill the glass with water. Pour slowly so the water doesn't spill. Now, do you think you can put some paper clips in the glass without the water spilling? Estimate how many clips you can put in. Try it! Put the clips in one at a time. What is happening to the water? How many clips did you put in before the water began to overflow? Start over and do the same experiment with pennies. Did you use more or less pennies? Why do think that happened?

Results

Fifty to one hundred paper clips or pennies can be added to the glass before it overflows.

Why?

Surface tension allows the water to expand and make room for the paper clips or pennies. This is called displacement.

Literature
The Trouble With Money
by Stan And Jan Berenstain

Sinking Water

Equipment

- clear container
- 4 identical small blocks of wood
- wax paper
- water

Procedure

Wrap two of the blocks of wood with wax paper. Put the two unwrapped blocks of wood close together on the water. What is happening to the blocks? Put the two wrapped blocks on the water. What happens to them? How is it different? What do you see if you look through the side of the container?

Results

The two unwrapped blocks move closer together. The water sticks to them and even moves itself up the sides. The two wrapped blocks don't come together and may push farther apart. They don't get wet.

Why?

The surface tension of the water between the un- wrapped blocks acts like a rubber band and pulls the blocks together. The wax paper around the wrapped blocks keeps the blocks from getting wet. It appears to make the blocks sink in the water. Look at the blocks through the side of the container to see this.

Literature

The Block
by Susan Aikin

47

Soap Propelled Boat

Equipment
- milk carton
- liquid soap
- eyedropper
- scissors
- tub of water

Procedure

Cut a boat out of the side of the milk carton. Make it four inches wide and seven inches long. Make the front a point and put a slot in the back. The slot should be in the center and be one and a half inches long and one inch wide. Put the boat in the water and try to make it go without touching it. Blow on it or make waves in the water. Is it moving? Put a drop of soap in the slot at the back. What happens to the boat? Now put several drops in the slot. What happens now? Does the boat move faster or slower? How far can you make the boat go?

Results

The boat moved forward when you dropped soap in the slot.

Why?

Remember, water likes to stick together. At the beginning, the boat stayed in one place because the water drops were pulling on it the same amount in every direction. Putting soap in the slot at the back weakens the strength of the water dops at the back of the boat. This makes the pull of the water in front of the boat stronger, so the water pulled the boat forward.

Literature
Boat Book
by Gail Gibbons

48

Side Or Center

Equipment

- wide mouthed, clear container
- pitcher or cup with a spout
- small cork or plastic bottle cap
- eyedropper

Procedure

Fill the container half full of water and drop the cork or lid into the water. Don't touch the cork or container but try to make the cork float in the center. Can you do it? Now, slowly pour water into the container using the pitcher. Keep pouring until the water is at the top of the container. Don't pour water on the cork and don't let the water overflow. Next, use the eyedropper and add a few drops of water at a time until the top bulges with water. What happens now? Do this experiment again and watch from the side of the container. Can you see how the water clings to the side and how it bulges over the top?

Results

The cork floats to the side when you first put it in the water and it stays on the side when you pour more water in the container. It is only when you use the eyedropper and the water is bulging that the cork goes to the center.

Why?

The cork stays on the side at the beginning because the water curves upward on the sides and the cork floats at the highest point. When the water bulged and curved upward in the center, the cork floated to the middle of the container because the center was the highest point. The cork will always float on the highest point.

Literature

Flying And Floating
by David Glover

49

Spurting Water

Equipment

- tin can
- nail
- hammer
- water

Procedure

Make three holes in the can near the bottom of the can with the hammer and the nail. They should be about 3/16 of an inch apart and in a row. Fill the can with water. The water will come spurting out the holes. Take your finger and thumb and pull them across the holes like you are pulling the streams of water together. What happens? Now cover the middle hole with your finger. Now what happens?

Results

When you pinch the spurts together, they will form one stream of water. When you covered the middle hole there were two spurts of water that merged into one.

Why?

Water likes to stick together. This is called cohesion. When the spurts stick together, surface tension (the film on the surface of the water) stops them from breaking apart.

Literature

Letting Swift River Go
by Jane Yolen

50

Stringing Water Along

Equipment
- 20 " piece of cotton string
- clear plastic drinking glass or container
- large dishpan or sink   • water
- measuring cup with spout and handle or pitcher

Procedure

Can string be used to fill a container with water? Set the drinking glass or container in the dishpan or sink. Wet the string. (Be sure to use string that will absorb water. Cotton string is best.) Tie one end of the string to the handle of the measuring cup or pitcher. Securely stretch the wet string from the measuring cup to the container. Carefully pour the water out of the pitcher so that it runs down the string. The string must be held tightly and the water poured slowly. What does the water do? Try it with a 36" piece of string.

Results

The water followed the string and dripped into the empty container.

Why?

The weight of the water pushes it down to the container on both pieces of string. The water adheres so solidly to the wet string that it doesn't fall off until it reaches the end. Surface tension is the reason the water clings to the string.

Literature
Berenstain Bears Science Fair

by Stan and Jan Berenstain

51

Powdery Pursuit

Equipment
- pie plate or round cake pan • water
- dishwashing liquid • rubber band
- baby powder • pepper
- sugar • cinnamon

Procedure

Put some water in the pie plate or cake pan. Ask the children to think about what might happen with the pepper, sugar, cinnamon, dish soap, and rubber band when they are put in the water. Do they think the items will float, sink, mix, or dissolve? What if items are combined and one or more are in the water at the same time? Have them compare their speculations with what really happens. Sprinkle pepper in the water. What happens? Add a drop of dish soap to the water. What happens now? Next, add some sugar to the water. What happens? Empty the water and try this again with the cinnamon and the rubber band. Did everything react the same way? Predict what would happen if you used baby powder. Try it and see.

Results
When the rubber band, cinnamon, and pepper are put in the water, they float. When the dish soap is added, the rubber band, cinnamon, and pepper "run away". When the sugar is added, the items "run back".

Why?
Any kind of soap added to the water weakens the surface tension and the ability of water to stick to itself. The sugar increases the power of the water to stick to itself. By adding sugar the water has a stronger ability to pull together.

Literature
Round Trip
by Ann Jonas

52

ENRICHMENT ACTIVITIES

Water Drops On a Penny

Get an eyedropper, a cup of water, some pennies and paper towels. Put a penny on a paper towel and drop water drops on the penny one at a time with the eyedropper. How many will go on the penny? Is it different if the other side of the penny is up? Can you pile drops on top of one another?

Surface Variety

What happens if you put the water drops on different surfaces? Do they behave the same way that they do on paper or freezer wrap? Try aluminum foil, regular paper, scraps of foil gift wrap or a Styrofoam meat tray.

Liquid Variety

What happens when you use different liquids or add different substances to the water? Try adding vinegar, salad oil, salt, sugar or anything else you can think of. What would happen if you use soda pop? Try both soda pop with bubbles and flat soda pop.

Look Again

Did you know that the curved surface of a water drop acts like a magnifying glass? How do your feet and fingers look under water? Look at them under the water when you take a bath. Lift them out of the water? Do they look different? Fill a round, tall, thin container half full of water. Put a ruler in it so that half of it is above the water and half of it is below the water. How does the ruler look? Now try it with a square container. Is the effect the same. Why or why not? The container alone does not make things look bigger.

Disappearing Coin

Put a cup on the table and put a coin inside it. Now walk back until you cannot see the coin. Have a friend pour water into the cup. What happens? Why did it happen?

When water is poured into the cup you can see the coin because water bends light rays and makes the coin seem higher up.

Vanishing Coin

Fill a big bowl with water. Put a coin in an empty glass and put the glass inside the bowl. Look at the glass from the side. What do you see? The coin has vanished. When an empty glass is surrounded by water, it is like a mirror. The reflection of the bowl on the sides of the glass makes the coin vanish. Now, fill the glass with water and the coin is back because the water in the glass stopped the bowl from being a mirror.

LEARNING ABOUT LIQUIDS

Liquids can be thin or thick, heavy or light, colored or clear. Some may form solids and others cause chemical reactions. All liquids can behave in magical ways. These experiments will explore some of the magic.

VOCABULARY

Talk about these words and what they mean as you do the experiments in this section. You can relate them specifically to the activity situation and then ask how they relate to cooking, repairing household items, and playing in the sand box.

VOCABULARY			
Words to use and define in this section are:			
top	press	bottom	through
mix	above	inside	separate
flat	solid	surface	sequence
poke	escape	outside	substance
half	liquid	combine	different
next	little	between	one-third
force			

LANGUAGE

You can use lots of description with these activities. Ask questions about why things are happening the way they are. Ask what would happen if one ingredient was left out.

PARENT NOTES

This is an opportunity for children to learn about substances that mix and substances that don't and to gain some understanding about the weight of liquids and gravity.

ACTIVITIES

- The Bewildering Bag
- Colors In A Bag
- Rainbow In A Bowl
- Porous Paper
- Levels of Liquid

LEARNING ABOUT LIQUIDS
The Bewildering Bag

Equipment
- plastic sandwich bag
- water
- pencils

Procedure
Fill the plastic sandwich bag with water and knot it or twist it and hold the top. Hold it over the sink. Push a pencil through one side of the bag. What happens? Why? Push another pencil through the bag. Now what happens. How many pencils can you push through the bag?

Results
The bag did not leak.

Why?
When you put the pencil through the lunch bag, the plastic pulls together around the pencil to close up the holes.

Literature
The Good Luck Pencil
by Diane Stanley

58

Colors In A Bag

Equipment
- 1 qt. plastic zip top bag
- cornstarch • water
- red, yellow and blue food coloring
- vegetable oil • tape

Procedure

Place the plastic bag so you can put things into it. Put in five tablespoons of cornstarch, a few drops of two primary colors, 1/2 cup water and 1/2 cup vegetable oil. Force the air out of the bag and seal it. Cover the sealed end with a wide strip of tape. Put it flat on the table and watch the colors mix and separate as you poke and press the contents. What is happening to the colors? Why do you think it is happening?

Results

The colors mix and then separate as the bag is manipulated.

Literature

Hailstones and Halibut Bones
by John Wallner

Why?

The cornstarch and food colors are soluble in water, so they mix. The oil is a greasy substance that is not soluble in water so it causes the designs in the bag as you poke the bag.

Rainbow In A Bowl

Equipment
- dark colored bowl
- water • toothpick
- 3 in 1 oil

Procedure

Put some water in the bowl. Wet the toothpick with oil and touch it to the top of the water in the bowl. Look at the surface from different points of view.

Results

Beautiful rainbow colors will be seen. Is this how a puddle looks after a rain? What makes puddles in the street look like this?

Why?

Light rays that hit the surface of the water are reflected off the oil and the water under the oil. As the oil moves it allows different colors to be seen.

Literature
A Rainbow Of My Own
by Don Freeman

60

Porous Paper

Equipment

- water
- paper lunch bag
- large paper grocery bag
- department store paper bag

Procedure

Will the paper bags hold water or will they leak? Fill each bag with about one inch of water. What happens? How are they different? Why do they act differently when they have water in them? Do the paper bags have a substance added to the paper to make them strong?

Results

All of the bags will hold water for a period of time. The bag made of the thinnest paper leaks or gets holes first. The bag of the heaviest paper leaks last.

Why?

The heavier paper is made to be stronger. Remember, grocery bags are made to carry heavy items.

Literature

The Paper Crane
by Molly Bang

Levels Of Liquid

Equipment
- molasses • tall glass
- pancake syrup
- rubbing alcohol
- cooking oil • water

Procedure

Fill the glass half full of water. Add about a 1/3 cup of alcohol. What happens? Add a little of the molasses. Now add the syrup. What is happening now? Next, add a little cooking oil. How does the glass look. Why is this happening?

Results

When the alcohol is added to the water, the water and alcohol mix. The molasses sinks to the bottom. The syrup is next. The oil floats on the top.

Why?

If substances do not mix, the heavier ones will sink and the lighter ones will float. The substances arranged themselves in sequence from heavy to light.

Literature

Raindrops and Rainbows
by Rose Wyler

62

ENRICHMENT ACTIVITIES

Dissolving

Make some hot tea and some iced tea. Put a spoonful of sugar in each. What happens? The sugar dissolves better in the hot tea than the cold tea. Why? Liquids can hold more solids when they are warm.

Gases

Pour a cold soft drink into a glass. Describe the way it looks and the bubbles of carbon dioxide. Now let it get warm. How does it look now? What happened? Liquids can hold more gases when they are cold.

Soluble Substances

Have an adult help with this experiment. Get some water, iodine, mineral oil and a jar with a tight fitting lid. Fill the jar half full of water. Add a few drops of iodine to make it light brown. Close the jar tightly and shake it. Open the jar and put in two or three tablespoons of the mineral oil. Tightly close the jar and shake it hard. Now let the jar sit for a few minutes. What is happening. Why do you think it is happening? The color left the water and went into the oil. This shows that some substances are more soluble in some liquids than others. (Vegetable oil does not work in this experiment.)

SINK AND FLOAT

Ask children about sinking and floating when they are swimming. Sinking is going beneath the surface of water and floating is being suspended on the surface of water. Adults will need to help children understand the idea that heavy and light alone do not make objects float or sink. It is the concept of heavy or light for the objects size. Even light stones sink. The heaviness of an object for its size is called its density. These experiments will give children the opportunity to explore and understand floating, sinking and density.

VOCABULARY

Use these words as you talk with the children about what they are doing. You don't need to "teach" them but just use them often as they are appropriate.

VOCABULARY			
Words to use and define in this section are:			
rim	float	better	combine
mix	lower	gently	predict
tip	press	inside	increase
sink	other	beneath	heaviest
push	heavy	surface	lightest
full	before	suspend	one-fourth
same	deeper	density	wrap around
tilt	volume	measure	three-fourths

KIDS KAPERS

LANGUAGE

Children should be encouraged to think about what the words sink and float mean. Ask them to consider what causes some objects to float, others to sink, and why a few will both float and sink. Prediction is a good activity for these experiments because there will be a lot of success with the predictions. There will also be surprises as well, which will make this section a lot of fun. Comparatives, using -er endings on words like bigger, smaller, and lighter, are valuable in this section. Superlatives (-est endings like heaviest) are also important in talking about these experiments.

PARENT NOTES

Help the children comprehend that surface tension and the coating on the water is what helps things float. They also need to grasp the concept of sink and float as best they can depending on their age. This will help them be able to predict what will sink or float, why things sink and float, and how they sink and float.

ACTIVITIES

- Oranges And Lemons
- Floating Pennies
- Sinking Cork
- Salty Sink Or Float
- Density Layers
- Hot And Cold
- The Hanging Egg
- Inside Outside

SINK AND FLOAT
Oranges And Lemons

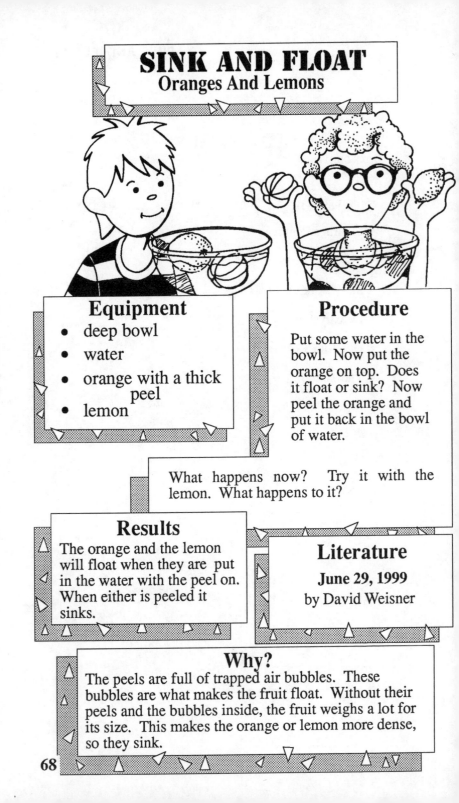

Equipment
- deep bowl
- water
- orange with a thick peel
- lemon

Procedure
Put some water in the bowl. Now put the orange on top. Does it float or sink? Now peel the orange and put it back in the bowl of water.

What happens now? Try it with the lemon. What happens to it?

Results
The orange and the lemon will float when they are put in the water with the peel on. When either is peeled it sinks.

Literature
June 29, 1999
by David Weisner

Why?
The peels are full of trapped air bubbles. These bubbles are what makes the fruit float. Without their peels and the bubbles inside, the fruit weighs a lot for its size. This makes the orange or lemon more dense, so they sink.

Floating Pennies

Procedure

Put the styrofoam cup in the water. Does it sink or float? Put a penny in the water. What does it do? Put a penny in the cup. Does the cup sink or float? Is the penny floating? How many pennies can you put in the cup before it sinks?

Add one penny at a time until water goes in the cup. How many pennies did you put in before the water started to go in the cup? You saw the penny sink in the water. How can you explain that a penny can float when it is in the cup?

Equipment

- deep bowl
- water
- styrofoam cup
- 100 pennies

Literature

Alexander Who Used To Be Rich Last Sunday
Judith Voirst

Results

As more pennies are added to the cup, it sinks deeper in the water. Finally, the water goes into the cup.

Why?

There is air in the cup and it will float as long as the weight of the cup is equal to the weight of the water that the cup pushes away. The increased weight of the pennies finally causes the cup to sink so deep that the water is able to go into the cup.

69

Sinking Cork

Equipment
- cork
- water
- clear plastic drinking glass
- plastic tub

Procedure

Put some water in the tub. Drop the cork in the water. Does it float or sink? Try to make it sink with your finger. What happens?

Hold the glass with its opening over the cork and gently lower the glass until its rim touches the bottom of the tub. What happens now?

Results

When you put the cork in the water it floats. You can't make it sink by pushing with your finger. As you put the glass over the cork and pushed it down into the water, did the cork sink? How did the glass make the cork sink?

Literature

Who Sank The Boat
by Pamela Allen

Why?

As the glass filled with water, the air in the glass was forced up toward the bottom of the glass. The air in the glass presses the cork to the bottom of the tub.

70

Salty Sink Or Float

Procedure

Put some tape on each jar for a label. Write "fresh" for fresh water on one jar, and "salt" on the other jar for salt water. Fill the jars about 3/4 full of water. Put the 10 tablespoons of salt into the jar labeled "salt." Stir it well. Clean the spoon. Is this water like the water in the ocean? How do you know?

Put the egg on the spoon and gently place it in the fresh water. Take the spoon away. What happens to the egg? Use the spoon to take the egg out of the fresh water and place it in the salt water. Carefully remove the spoon. What happens to the egg now? What does this experiment show? Will this happen to other objects if you put them in fresh and salt water? Try it!

Equipment

- 2--16oz. wide mouth jars
- 10 tablespoons of salt
- spoon to stir with
- fresh egg • water
- tape • marking pen
- spoon large enough to hold egg

Literature

Salt

by Norma Bracy

Results

The egg will sink in fresh water and it will float in the salt water.

Why?

The salt in the water pushes objects to the surface. See if you can figure out how heavy an object can be and still float in the jar used for this experiment?

71

Density Layers

Equipment

- 3 small clear plastic glasses (all the same)
- dark corn syrup (so you can see it better)
- food coloring • cooking oil
- spoon to stir with • water
- measuring cup
- small scale to weigh the glasses

Procedure

Measure 1/4 cup of water and pour it into one of the glasses. Dry the measuring cup. Measure 1/4 cup cooking oil and put it into another glass. Wash the measuring cup with soap and water and dry it. Now put 1/4 cup corn syrup in the last glass. Which liquid do you think is the heaviest? Which is the lightest? How would you discover the heaviest and lightest? Add a few drops of the food coloring to the water and stir it to mix it. Carefully pour the water into the oil glass. Now pour the corn syrup into the glass with the water and oil. What happens? Do the substances mix? Which is more dense? How do you know?

Results

When you combine the liquids in the glasses, the oil will float on the water and the corn syrup sinks to the bottom showing that the oil is lightest and the syrup the heaviest.

Literature

As Old As The Hills
by Melvin Berger

Why?

The oil is the lightest, so it floats on the top of the glass. It is less dense than water. The corn syrup is the heaviest. It sinks to the bottom of the glass because it is more dense than water.

Hot And Cold

Procedure

Fill the bowl with very cold water. Fill the bottle with hot water. Leave enough room for a few drops of food coloring and put the food coloring in the water in the bottle. Hold your thumb or finger over the top of the bottle and gently put it into the bowl of cold water.

Gently take your finger off the bottle and let the water flow out. Very slowly take your hand out of the bowl. What happens? Do this experiment again but this time put the hot water in the bowl and the cold water and food coloring in the bottle. Now what happens? Does cold water mix with warm water?

Equipment

- mixing bowl
- small clear bottle
- food coloring
- marking pen or crayon
- hot and cold tap water

Literature

Hot As An Ice Cube
by Philip Balestrino

Results

When the hot water in the bottle is added to the cold water in the bowl, the hot water floats at first. When the cold water from the bottle is mixed with the hot water in the bowl, the cold water sinks at first. In both experiments, the water mixes as the water temperatures get closer together. Based on this acitvity, do hot and cold water weigh the same or is one heavier and therefore more dense than the other?

Why?

The cold water is more dense than the hot water. It will move to the bottom because of this density. The water mixes when the temperature of the hot and cold water become the same.

The Hanging Egg

Equipment
- egg
- wide mouth glass
- water
- measuring cup
- 1/2 cup salt
- crayon
- spoon to stir with

Procedure

Fill the glass with three ounces of water from the measuring cup. Add the salt and stir it well. Use the crayon to draw a face on the egg. Tip the glass gently and pour three ounces of cold water from the measuring cup on top of the salt water. Carefully put the egg in the glass.

What happens? Try putting food coloring in each container of water. Now what happens?

Results

The egg should sink through the plain water and sit on the salt water. It is hanging in the middle of the glass.

Literature

Eggs-O-Poppin
by Carol Nicklaus

Why?

The salt water is more dense than the egg or the plain water so both the egg and the plain water float.

Inside Outside

Procedure

Fill the bowl with water. Make a small amount of the clay into a ball. What will the clay ball do when you put it into the water? Try it and see. What will the block do when you put it into the water? Did it do what you predicted?

Equipment

- glass bowl
- water
- clay
- small wooden block

How can you get the clay to float? Can you use the wooden block to make the clay float? Wrap the clay around the block so it covers the outside in the shape of a ball. The wooden block will be on the inside. What happens when you put the clay wrapped block into the water?

Results

The clay ball sank to the bottom of the tub. The block floated. When the block was inside the clay ball, it floated.

Literature

Outside Inside Poems
by Arnold Adoff

Why?

The wooden block inside the clay ball continued to be lighter than water so it assisted in holding up the clay ball. The piece of wood made the size of the clay ball bigger, even if it was the same amount of clay. When the clay ball became bigger, it spread its weight out over the water which enabled it to float.

KIDS KAPERS

ENRICHMENT ACTIVITIES

Eggs Up

Fill a large bowl with water. Add four tablespoons of salt and stir it to mix it. Put three or four raw eggs in the water. Do they float? Keep adding salt. What happens? Which end of the eggs is up? Why? Hard boil an egg and peel it as if you were going to eat it. What do you see at the top of the egg? The egg floats with the bigger end up because there is an air pocket there. You can see the air pocket when you peel your hard boiled egg.

Mixtures

When you experimented with hot and cold water, did you think of times in the environment when hot and cold water mix? Think of that now. What about rain or snow? What happens when cold water from melting snow flows into warm water lakes? Does the water mix. What about oil spills in lakes or oceans? Do oil and water mix? What do the ocean waves do to an oil spill? What do oil spills do to birds, fish and animals?

Vegetables and Fruits

Which vegetables and fruits will float and which will sink? Try an onion, grape, strawberry, potato, apple, carrot, tomato or any other one you may like.

Clay and Sticks

Can you make a clay ball float using craft or popsicle sticks? How would you do it? How many sticks would you use? How would you put them in the clay? Try putting them in like the rays of the sun. Try this with toothpicks. Will it work? Why or why not?

What Will Float?

Gather a group of objects and see which ones float and which ones sink. Try a paper clip, plastic lid, rubber band, plastic fork, sponge, twist tie, scrap of fabric, leaf, cotton,

76

piece of ivory soap, crayon, pencil or anything else you want to try.

Up or Down?

Put a cup right side up on a bowl of water. What happens? Now turn the cup upside down. What happen this time? The cup that is right side up floats, the upside down cup sinks. Some things sink or float depending on how they are placed in the water.

ICE

What do you think of when you think of ice? Do you think of ice cubes in a frosty glass, icicles hanging from the roof in the winter, or people skating on a frozen pond? Ice is water in it's solid state. Ice is fascinating to explore and play with and is an easy substance to make. Ice forms when water freezes. It is made up of crystals, but the crystals are so close together you can't tell where one ends and one begins.

VOCABULARY

When you are introducing the words for the experiments, children need to understand what they mean in the context of each experiment. Since many words can have more than one meaning, the way they're used for each experiment needs to be discussed.

VOCABULARY			
Words to use and define in this section are:			
mark	twist	colder	crushed
same	equal	across	coldest
cold	third	heavier	spread out
level	gather	lighter	three-quarters
pinch	amount		

LANGUAGE

This unit lends itself well to learning and using new vocabulary. As you talk about the ice and handle it, you can use synonyms as descriptive words. For example, you can say the ice is frigid, frosty, or slippery. The freezer is subzero, arctic, and freezing. You could make a game of thinking of all the words you know with ice in them - ice cream, ice box, ice chest, ice field, ice cold, ice boat, ice machine, iceberg, ice pack, ice pick, ice water, or ice storm which could lead to discussions of all those words and learning more vocabulary and language. Use the new vocabulary in new ways. For example, say or write a poem.

Ice
freezing, slippery,
frosty, frigid,
popping, melting,
hard water,
cold as cold,
Ice

PARENT NOTES

These activities can be done in the summer and again in the winter with different results if you do them outside. As part of this group of experiments, you could go for a walk when the ice crust has formed over puddles and make a language lesson when the children step on that ice and it breaks and shatters. In the summer, children can be captivated by just playing with an ice cube. You might want to use that play as a "warm up" for the projects in this unit. Use your imagination and think up some icy activities that your children would enjoy.

ACTIVITIES

- Through The Ice
- What's The Water Level
- Holey Ice
- Bigger Water
- Oil And Ice
- Ice, Salt, and Sugar
- Melting Ice
- Measuring The Cold

ICE
Through The Ice

Equipment
- piece of thin wire 8" long
- sticky tape
- plastic soda bottle
- spoons for weights
- ice cube

Procedure

Twist each end of the wire around the handles of two spoons and secure them with tape. Balance the ice cube on the top of the bottle. Put the wire across the top of the cube so the spoons hang down equally on each side. What is going to happen? Did your prediction happen?

Results
The wire on top sinks through the ice and then the ice forms over the wire again.

Why?
The pressure of the spoons pulling the wire down lowers the melting point of the ice. The ice changes to water where the wire presses on it.

Literature
Snow And Ice
by Joy Palmer

What's The Water Level?

Equipment
- a clear glass
- water
- ice cube
- food coloring
- marker or tape

Procedure

Put some water in the glass. Add a drop of food coloring. Mark the water level with some tape or a marker. Add an ice cube. Where will the water level be when the ice cube melts? What will happen if you put in two ice cubes?

Results

Part of the ice cube floats above the water in the glass. The water level is the same before and after the ice melts.

Literature
It Could Still Be Water
by Allan Fowler

Why?

When the ice melts, the water from it takes up less space than the ice.

Holey Ice

Equipment
- shallow bowl
- salt
- ice cube

Procedure

Put the ice cube in the bowl. Put a pinch of salt on the ice cube. Put it in a cool, safe place for about ten minutes. What happens to the ice cube? Why is it happening?

Results

The place on the ice cube where you put the salt changes into water while the rest of the ice cube stays frozen.

Why?

Ice does not melt until it reaches it's melting point of 32 degrees farenheit. When you add salt to the ice it lowers the melting point of the ice below 32 degrees. The result is that the salty middle melts due to a lower melting point and the rest stays frozen because it's melting point is still 32 degrees.

Literature
Icebergs and Glaciers
by Seymour Simon

84

Bigger Water

Equipment

- clear glass
- water
- tray of ice cubes

Procedure

Fill the glass with water to the top so it's really full, but not overflowing. Add a handful of ice cubes. What happens? Now try this-put a handful of ice cubes in the glass and then fill it with water. Wait for the ice cubes to melt. What happens to the water level? What did you think would happen?

Results

When you dropped the ice cubes in the container of water, the water level rose or the glass overflowed. When the ice cubes that were put in first melted, the water level didn't change.

Why?

When it freezes, water does something very interesting-it gets bigger! When water is frozen into an ice cube, it takes up space like a toy block and pushes water out of the glass. When it melts, it gets smaller again so the water level goes back down.

Literature

A Tale Of Antartica
by Ulco Glimmerveen

Oil And Ice

Equipment

- jar or glass
- cooking oil
- ice cubes
- metal ice cube tray

Procedure

Fill the jar or glass 3/4 full of cooking oil. Gently place an ice cube on the top of the oil. Watch it melt. What do you think will happen? What do the water drops do as they melt? Is water heavier or lighter than the oil? How can you make an ice cube that's heavier than oil? Try adding food coloring to the water and freeze the mixture in a metal ice cube tray. (It will stain a plastic tray.) How much food coloring do you need to add before the ice cube sinks?

Results

The water floats when it is frozen but sinks when it melts.

Why?

When water is frozen and in a solid state it is lighter than oil. Its molecules expand into ice crystals that take up more space than liquid. When it melts, and it is a liquid, it's heavier than oil.

Literature

Professor Puffendorf's Secret Potions
by Robin Tzannes & Korky Paul

Ice, Salt, And Sugar

Equipment

- ice block (frozen in a quart milk carton)
- 3 tablespoons table salt
- 2 tablespoons sugar
- 2 tablespoons rock salt
- food coloring

Procedure

You should do this experiment outside or in a plastic tub to catch the melting water. Take the ice block out of the carton. Put it in the tub. Put two tablespoons of the rock salt in one spot. In another spot, pour three tablespoons of table salt. Find another spot and put two tablespoons of sugar there. In the last spot, put a few drops of food coloring. What is happening in each spot? How is each spot the same? How are they different? Draw a picture to show what is happening.

Results

The different kinds of salt melt into the ice block in different designs. Some spots melt faster than others. The food coloring colors the ice crystals.

Literature

Ralph's Frozen Tale
by Elise Primavera

Why?

The salt melts the ice because the salt lowers the freezing point of water. The food coloring colors the ice crystals that are already there.

Melting Ice

Equipment

- 4 clear plastic drinking glasses
- glass of snow (if available)
- glass of crushed ice   • water
- glass of ice cubes

Procedure

Put one cup of water in one of the glasses. In another glass, put the ice cubes. In the third glass, put the crushed ice. Put the snow in the last glass. Let the ice in the glasses melt. Will the glasses have the same amount of water as the water glass? Will they be full? Will they be less than full or will they overflow?

Results

The full glasses of ice cubes, crushed ice or snow will melt to be less than a full glass of water.

Why?

Ice molecules expand and take up more space than liquid. It takes nine to ten glasses of snow to equal one glass of water.

Literature

Changes
by Anthony Browne

Measuring The Cold

Equipment
- 4 tablespoons table or rock salt
- 3 clear plastic glasses • paper towels
- tape you can write on • 12 ice cubes
  - unbreakable, alcohol liquid measure thermometer
    - measuring cup • water
      - pen or crayon

Procedure
Put a piece of tape on each glass. Using the pen or crayon label the glasses with 1, 2 and 3. Put four ice cubes in glass 1. Put four ice cubes and 1/2 cup of water in glass 2. In glass 3, put 4 ice cubes, 1/2 cup water, and the 4 tablespoons of salt. Wait a few minutes. Test the temperature of the water with your finger and mark the glasses in order from least cold to coldest. Now, measure the temperature of the water with the thermometer. Which glass is the coldest? Why do you think that is?

Results
Glass 1 is cold, glass 2 is colder, and glass 3 is the coldest.

Why?
Plain ice that melts to plain water is cold, so glass 1 is cold. When salt is mixed with ice, it forms a mixture with a lower freezing point than water, so glass 2 is colder. A mixture of ice, salt, and water makes salt brine. Salt brine is colder than ice or ice water, so glass 3 is the coldest.

Literature
The Sugar Snow Spring
by Lillian Hoban

ENRICHMENT

Ice Shapes

Freeze water in different shaped containers. Use half pint milk cartons, gallon milk containers, margarine containers, and others of your choice. When they are all frozen, unwrap them and put them outside. Which one will melt first? Why? To find out, draw a picture of what they look like and write down the time you put them outside. Check them often and write down the time they are melted.. Which ones melt faster? What do some of the shapes have in common? How are they different?

Facts About Ice

Freeze water in an ice cube tray. Gather some different substances like sand, gravel, salt, wax paper, a towel, tin foil, and toilet paper. Take the cubes outside and take them out of the ice cube tray. Spread them out and surround each one with the different materials. Write down the time it takes each one to melt. Which things cause ice to melt quickly? Which things keep ice frozen longer?

Icicles

Icicles form at the edge of the roof as the sun turns snow to water and later the cold turns it back to ice. Are icicles always on the same side of the building? Does their length differ in various locations?

BALLOONS

Balloons are some of the greatest toys for having fun. We all think of round ones as party decorations and we all know that long skinny ones can be twisted into animal shapes. We can even remember a hot, sunny day when we used them as water bombs. They are also one of the greatest tools for learning about science. Using balloons for science experiments will help you learn about the properties of gases and the concepts of force and pressure. Do you know how these properties relate to what happens in the world? Get a balloon, try these activities, and find out.

VOCABULARY

VOCABULARY			
Words to use and define in this section are:			
pour	flat	center	gently
near	half	soften	through
boil	punch	middle	stretch
vent	front	escape	suspend
over	cover	inside	between
tube	piece	secure	different
back			

LANGUAGE

These activities are an opportunity for a lot of verbal sharing. For example, talk about and carefully show boiling water (a chance for a safety lesson as well) and how you got the water in the bottle. Did you use a funnel or do it over the sink to catch spills? Talk a lot about vinegar and baking soda and what happens when they mix. You could use those substances to explore proportions - how much soda or vinegar do you need to make it explode? Make a volcano with a bottle in the center in a paper maiche mountain and make it erupt with vinegar and baking soda. You could add red food coloring to make the eruption fiery. The important thing is to ask questions, discuss, and talk, talk, talk.

PARENT NOTES

Balloons are great for having fun, but they are also marvelous tools for science. You can make lots of wonderful discoveries with balloons. They will prove strange but true facts about the world around you. Help the children relate what they see with the balloon activities to what happens in the world by describing experiments and asking appropriate questions. When balloons break, save the pieces in a safe place for other experiments in this book. One word of caution -keep very young children safe by not allowing them to play with the balloons.

ACTIVITIES

- Blowing Up
- Up The Balloon
- Sinking Balloons
- Suspended Balloon
- Balloon In A Bottle
- Speeding Balloon
- Shrinking Balloon
- Heavy Air

BALLOONS
Blowing Up

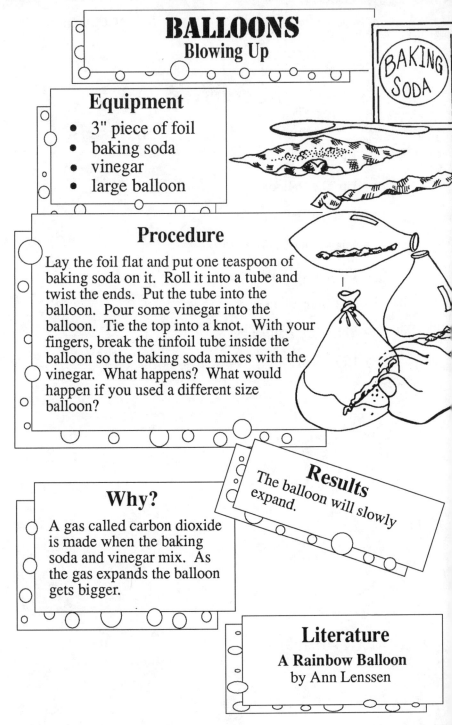

Equipment

- 3" piece of foil
- baking soda
- vinegar
- large balloon

Procedure

Lay the foil flat and put one teaspoon of baking soda on it. Roll it into a tube and twist the ends. Put the tube into the balloon. Pour some vinegar into the balloon. Tie the top into a knot. With your fingers, break the tinfoil tube inside the balloon so the baking soda mixes with the vinegar. What happens? What would happen if you used a different size balloon?

Results

The balloon will slowly expand.

Why?

A gas called carbon dioxide is made when the baking soda and vinegar mix. As the gas expands the balloon gets bigger.

Literature

A Rainbow Balloon
by Ann Lenssen

Up The Balloon

Equipment
- 2 liter plastic soda bottle
- bucket that will hold the bottle
- hot water (an adult must help with the hot water)
- cold water • balloon

Procedure

Fill the bottle about half way up with the cold water. Blow up the balloon and let the air out of it. This will soften and stretch it. Put the balloon over the top of the bottle. Pour the hot water into the bucket (have an adult help with the hot water) and put the bottle with the balloon on top into the bucket. Keep watching the balloon. What is happening? What if the bucket was full of cold water instead of hot water?

Results

The balloon will stand up when the cold water bottle is put in the hot water bucket. When the cold water bottle is put into the cold water bucket, nothing happens.

Why?

When the cold water bottle is put into the hot water, the air inside the bottle gets warmer. Warm air takes up more space than cold air, so the air moves into the balloon making it stand up.

Literature

**Miss Eva And
The Red Balloon**
by Karen M. Glennon

Sinking Balloons

Equipment

- small can
- piece of rubber balloon
- water • tape
- nail • hammer
  - rubber band

Procedure

Use the hammer and nail to punch a hole in the can near the bottom. Cover the hole with the tape. Fill the can with water. Stretch the rubber balloon piece over the top of the can and secure it with the rubber band. Go outside and put the can in the grass or hold the can over the sink or tub. Take off the tape. What happens to the water and the balloon?

Results

As the water comes out of the can, the balloon is sucked into the can.

Why?

The air pressure forces the balloon into the can as the water leaves the can.

Literature

The Highest Balloon On The Common

by Carol Carrick

Suspended Balloon

Equipment

- balloon
- heater vent in the floor

Procedure

Blow up the balloon and tie it so the air stays in. Put the balloon over the vent when the air is blowing out. What happens? Ask an adult to help and use the blower on the vacuum cleaner to suspend the balloon. Is it the same as the heater vent? Does the balloon move up and down?

Results

The balloon seems suspended in the air. It may move up and down depending on the force of the blowing air.

Why?

The air rising from the register or vacuum suspends the balloon. If the balloon moves away from the place where the air is rising, the slower moving air pushes it back. The up and down motion is due to the upward push from the blowing air and the downward force of gravity.

Literature

Hot Air Henry

by Mary Calhoun

Balloon In A Bottle

Equipment
- 2 liter bottle without the lid
- balloon
- very hot water
  (an adult must help with this)

Procedure

An adult needs to help boil the water. Pour the boiling water into the bottle. Shake it around to warm the bottle and pour it out. Quickly put the balloon over the top of the bottle. Watch what happens.

Results
The balloon gets pushed into the bottle.

Why?

Less space is used by the steam and moisture as the bottle cools. As the pressure in the bottle is reduced, the pressure of the outside air inflates the balloon and pushes it inside the bottle.

Literature

Up Goes Mr. Downs
by Jerry Smith

Speeding Balloon

Equipment

- medium or large balloon
- drinking straw
- string or yarn • tape

Procedure

Put the string through the straw. If you have three people, have one person hold one end of the string and another person hold the other end. Otherwise, tie the string between two chairs. You decide how long the string should be. Blow up the balloon, hold the top closed, and gently tape it to the straw at the front and the back. Have the open end of the balloon next to a chair or a person. Let go of the balloon so the air comes out of it. What happens? How far do you think the balloon will travel? Would a larger balloon go farther?

Results

The straw and the balloon speed down the string.

Why?

The trapped air in the balloon speeds out and makes the balloon go along the string.

Literature

The Big Balloon Race

by Eleanor Coerr

Shrinking Balloons

Equipment

- balloon
- string
- the freezer part of the refrigerator

Procedure

Blow up the balloon and tie it so the air stays in. Tie a string around the middle of the balloon. Put the balloon in the freezer for ten or fifteen minutes. What is happening in the freezer? Is the balloon freezing like ice? When the time is up take the balloon out of the freezer. What do you see? Why did it happen? What will happen if you leave the balloon in the room? Try it and see.

Results

The string is loose and the balloon is smaller.

Why?

Heat takes up space. Cold takes up less space. As the balloon got colder it got smaller. As the balloon warmed up in the room it got big again.

Literature

A Balloon For Grandad

by Nigel Gray

Heavy Air

Equipment

- 2 balloons the same size
- stick about 18" long
- string

Procedure

Tie the string in the center of the stick. Tie the other end of the string to a tree branch, clothesline, or something else to suspend it. Center the string in the middle of the stick so it balances. Tie a flat balloon to each end of the stick. Remove one of the balloons, blow air into it, and tie it so it won't leak. Now tie it back onto the end of the stick. What happens to the end of the stick with the blown up balloon? Why?

Results

The balloon with the air pulls the stick down.

Why?

The air in the balloon is heavy so it makes the balloon heavier. The heavy balloon makes that end of the stick move down and not balance.

Literature

Air Is All Around You

by Franklyn M. Branley

ENRICHMENT

Sticking Balloons

   Blow up a balloon and tie it. Rub it on a carpet, a wool sweater or your hair. Hold the balloon against the wall. What happens? Blow up some more balloons and rub them too. Set the balloons on the table. Do they move toward each other or away from each other? Mix some salt and pepper and put it on a plate. Rub your balloon again and put it over the salt and pepper. What moves? Why? When you rub the balloons they get charged with static electricity. What happens if you leave the balloons alone? Can you charge them up again?

Curving Water

   Blow up a balloon and tie it. Rub it on a wool sweater or something else to give it static electricity. Turn on the water in the sink and hold the charged balloon near the running water. The water is attracted toward the charged balloon and you can see the water curve toward it.

Balloon On A Bottle

   Take the lid off a plastic soda bottle. Put the bottle in the freezer for about fifteen minutes. Blow up a small balloon, then let the air out of it. This will stretch and loosen it. Take the bottle out of the freezer and put the balloon over the opening. Rub the bottle to warm it up. What will the balloon do?

Bubbles From A Balloon

   Blow up a balloon. Hold the end together so no air leaks out. Fill a tub with water. Put the balloon under the water and let go of the end. Are there bubbles? As the air escapes it makes air bubbles in the water.

Boats With Balloons

   Cut a milk or juice carton in half from top to bottom to make a boat. Use the part of the carton that has the sealed top for the front of the boat. Poke a hole in the rear of the boat (the bottom part) and put the balloon top through the hole. Blow up the balloon, hold the air in it and put your boat in the tub. Let the balloon go and your boat will go too.

Lift with a balloon

Put a balloon on a table with the open end off the table. Put a book on the balloon. Blow up the balloon. What is happening to the book? As you put air into the balloon it needs someplace to go, so the air pressure in the balloon lifts the book.

Balloon Scents

When you leave a balloon overnight, you can tell that it begins to lose air. Pour a drop of perfume, after shave, scented dish soap, vinegar or other substance that smells into the balloon. Blow it up and tie it. As you leave it overnight it will smell.

JUST FOR FUN

The experiments in this section come from a variety of areas and are truly Just For Fun! Some of these activities children will want to do again and again. A few will result in a product they will have to show everyone. These are the projects children will want to illustrate or write about. Adults, you will enjoy doing these experiments too!

VOCABULARY

These vocabulary words are used throughout the experiments listed in this section. Read through the experiments before beginning to identify which words belong with each experiment. Explain what the words mean as you use them in the experiment. They will have different meanings for the children depending on their age.

VOCABULARY			
Words to use and define in this section are:			
rim	across	through	separate
half	strong	compare	sprinkle
third	remove	fragile	substance
bounce	pattern	preserve	invisible
fourth	visible	pressure	kaleidoscope

LANGUAGE

These experiments come from a variety of areas and therefore lend themselves to understanding many language skills. In this section you can ask "what happens next" and "what happens if" questions. Have students compare and contrast the activities in this section with each other and with the other experiments they have done. Children can answer why, what and how questions, and they can describe the products they have made and the sequence they used to make them.

PARENT NOTES

Remember to keep all of the activities fun. When children have an enjoyable time learning, they will develop a lifetime love of learning. It is a good idea to concentrate on only one area of language during each experiment to help children focus on one skill at a time. A few of these experiments involve money. This gives you and the children the opportunity to use the abundance of children's literature to learn about money.

ACTIVITIES

- Bursting Milk
- Lively Popcorn
- More Lively Popcorn
- Magnet Pictures
- Flexible Bones
- Pepper
- Flying Coins
- Pepper And Salt
- Invisible Ink
- Writing With Wax
- Water That Won't Pour
- Measuring The Rain
- Manufacturing Snowflakes
- Hole In A Bottle
- Is It Acid Rain?
- Its Leaking!
- Oxidation
- Slippery Solution

JUST FOR FUN
Bursting Milk

Equipment

- milk
- food coloring
- cereal bowl
- dishwashing liquid

Procedure

Pour a little milk into the dish. Add a drop of one color of food coloring. Watch carefully as you do the next step. Put a drop of dishwashing liquid on the color. What is happening? Why is this experience called Bursting Milk? Try it with more than one color drop on the milk. What happens now?

Results

When the soap is added to the milk, the color bursts to the sides of the bowl. Sometimes it makes a pattern like a kaleidoscope.

Why?

Food coloring is watery. The milk has some fat in it. When the dishwashing liquid touches the milk, it breaks up the fat pieces and makes them spread out. This mixes the food coloring and the milk.

Literature

Make Me A Peanut Butter Sandwich And A Glass Of Milk by Ken Robbins

Lively Popcorn

Equipment

- clear glass
- water
- popcorn kernels
- 2 antacid tablets

Procedure

This is a good experiment to write or draw about because it happens in visible steps. Fill the glass with 3/4 cup water. Drop in a few popcorn kernels. What happens? Add two antacid tablets. Now what happens? Keep watching and observing. Are things changing? What does this experiment show?

Results

As the antacid works, the popcorn floats to the top. As time goes on, the kernels go up and down..

Why?

Antacid tablets contain citric acid and sodium bicarbonate. When they mix with water, these two substances make carbon dioxide. The carbon dioxide bubbles stick to the popcorn kernels and make them rise to the top.

Literature
Sing A Song Of Popcorn
by Beatrice Schenk de Regniers

109

More Lively Popcorn

Equipment
- clear glass
- baking soda
- vinegar
- food coloring
- popcorn kernels

Procedure

Put water in the glass. Add one tablespoon of baking soda and a few drops of food coloring. Stir the mixture. Add some popcorn kernels and stir in three tablespoons of vinegar. What happens to the popcorn? Can you make the kernels bounce again? How would you do it? Try adding more baking soda.

Results

The popcorn kernels rise to the top and then sink. When more baking soda is added, they rise again.

Why?

The baking soda and vinegar mix and form carbon dioxide. The carbon dioxide bubbles stick to the popcorn kernels and pull them to the top of the glass. When the bubbles pop, the popcorn sinks again.

Literature
The Popcorn Book
by Tomie dePaola

Magnet Pictures

Equipment
- magnet
- salt
- iron filings
- white cardboard
- spray bottle
- can of spray paint

Procedure

Set the magnet on a flat surface. Put the card over the magnet. Sprinkle the iron filings on the card. Gently tap the card until the iron filings make the pattern of the force of the magnet. One way you can preserve the pattern is to spray salt water on the iron filings. Spray them again after a few hours. Let them sit overnight. The next morning, carefully remove the magnet and dump the iron filings on another piece of paper. Another way you can save the pattern is to spray the card lightly with a dark colored spray paint. When the paint dries, remove the magnet and iron filings as before.

Results

The salt water spray makes a rust pattern on the white cardboard and the spray paint makes a white pattern on a dark background.

Why?

The salt water rusts the iron filings so the pattern is in rust. The spray paint covers the surface where the iron filings were and leaves that pattern.

Literature
Look At Magnets
by Rena Kirkpatrick

111

Flexible Bones

Equipment

- vinegar
- container with a cover or a glass
- small chicken bone (a wishbone works best)

Procedure

Put the chicken bone in the container. Fill it with enough vinegar to cover the bone. Let it soak for two days. Pour off the vinegar and add some fresh vinegar. Let it soak for two more days. What is happening to the bone? Try this with an egg Let the egg soak overnight. The shell on the egg is like the enamel on our teeth. Does acid in food make the enamel on teeth disappear? Is this how we get cavities?

Results

The bone becomes soft and flexible. The shell of the egg completely disappears.

Why?

Bones are made of hard materials such as calcuim and a soft material called collagen. The acid in the vinegar dissolved the calcium which is hard, and left the collagen which is soft. Egg shells are made of calcium so they completely disappear.

Literature

Skinny Bones
by Barbara Parks

Pepper

Equipment

- glass
- water
- soap
- shaker of pepper

Procedure

Fill the glass with water. Sprinkle pepper on the top of the water so that it covers the top. Move your finger across the water through the pepper. What happens to the pepper? Rinse and dry your finger. Now, rub it on the soap and move it across the water through the pepper again. What happened this time? Why do you think this happened?

Results

When you have no soap on your finger, the pepper closes in behind your finger as it moves. When the soap is on your finger, the pepper stays apart.

Why?

Without the soap, the surface tension draws the pepper to cover the top of the water after your finger goes through it. The soap on your finger weakens the surface tension of the water so that it doesn't pull back together.

Literature

Sometimes Things Change
by Patricia Eastman

113

Flying Coins

Equipment
- coin
- small bottle
- petroleum jelly

Procedure

Put the bottle in the freezer for about five minutes. Take it out and spread some petroleum jelly around the top. Set a coin on the top and warm the bottle by rubbing it up and down and around the sides. Keep rubbing. What do you think will happen? Did your prediction come true?

Results

The coin suddenly popped up.

Why?

The air inside the bottle heats up and as it expands it pushes the coin off the top.

Literature

The Lost Coin
by Debbie O'Neal &
Amelia Rosato

Pepper And Salt

Equipment

- spoon
- bowl or piece of wax paper
- salt • pepper

Procedure

Mix a little salt and pepper together and put it in the bowl or on the wax paper. Take the spoon and try to separate the pepper from the salt. Can you do it? Now take the spoon and rub it on your hair or a sweater made of manmade fibers. Now try to separate the pepper from the salt. Can you predict what will happen? Why do you think this happened?

Results

It is, of course, impossible to separate the pepper from the salt with a spoon. After rubbing the spoon, the pepper moves up from the salt and clings to the spoon.

Why?

By rubbing the spoon on your hair or the sweater you give it static electricity. The pepper is light and the electricity on the spoon lifts it away from the salt.

Literature

Grains Of Salt
by Dominique Joly

115

Invisible Ink

Equipment
- white paper
- lemon
- potato · glass
- onion · toothpicks

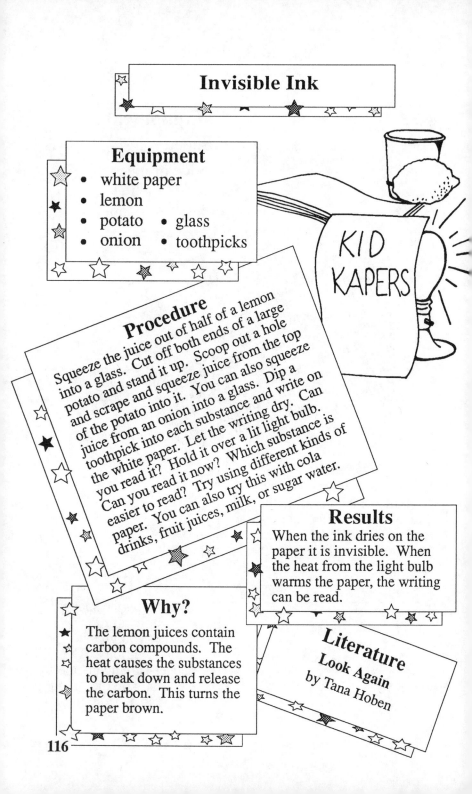

Procedure
Squeeze the juice out of half of a lemon into a glass. Cut off both ends of a large potato and stand it up. Scoop out a hole and scrape and squeeze juice from the top of the potato into it. You can also squeeze juice from an onion into a glass. Dip a toothpick into each substance and write on the white paper. Let the writing dry. Can you read it? Hold it over a lit light bulb. Can you read it now? Which substance is easier to read? Try using different kinds of paper. You can also try this with cola drinks, fruit juices, milk, or sugar water.

Results
When the ink dries on the paper it is invisible. When the heat from the light bulb warms the paper, the writing can be read.

Why?
The lemon juices contain carbon compounds. The heat causes the substances to break down and release the carbon. This turns the paper brown.

Literature
Look Again
by Tana Hoben

Writing With Wax

Equipment
- candle
- white paper
- pencil or pen
- instant coffee or cocoa powder

Procedure

Rub the candle over the paper to make it waxy. Put the paper wax side down on top of another sheet of paper. Write your message using firm pressure so that it goes on the paper underneath. Remove the waxy paper. Can you read the message? Now sprinkle the powdered substance over the writing. Can you read your note now?

Results

Any powdered substance will stick to the wax and allow the message to be read.

Literature
Messages In The Mailbox
by Loreen Leedy

Why?

The powdered substance will stick to the wax and allow the message to be read.

Water That Won't Pour

Equipment

- piece of cardboard
- water • coffee mug
- pitcher or cup with a spout

Procedure

Do this activity over a sink, bucket, or large bowl. Cut the cardboard into a 4 1/2" square. Fill the mug with water. Put in enough water to make it bulge over the top of the mug but not spill. Place the cardboard firmly over the mug of water and turn the mug upside down. Hold the cardboard firmly for a few seconds and then take your hand away. What happens? Does the water spill out? If it does, put more water in the mug and try again. How long can you hold the mug upside down without the water spilling out?

Results

The cardboard sticks on the mug and holds the water in the mug. It doesn't spill out.

Why?

By filling the cup just to the point of spilling and putting the cardboard on firmly, a vacuum is created. The vacuum holds the cardboard on and the water in.

Literature

Water
by Francois Michel

Measuring The Rain

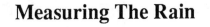

Equipment

- coffee can
- pen or marker
- funnel as wide as the coffee can
- tall thin bottle with straight sides (try an empty pill container)
- ruler or measuring tape

Procedure

Mark off one inch on the side of the can. Fill it with water to the one inch line. Pour this amount of water into the tall thin bottle and mark the bottle at the one inch line. Take the ruler and mark the inch into eighths. Use the pen or marker and make the marks on the side of the bottle. Now, wait for rain. You need an open, flat area in your front or back yard. Set out the can with the funnel on top.

Results

The funnel will catch the raindrops that fall on its rim and help them get into the can. When the rain has stopped, bring in the can and pour the water into the bottle you have marked with the measurements. Read the amount of rain. Compare the amount of rain you have with the amount the weather forecaster gives.

Why?

The funnel directs the raindrops onto the can. Then you can measure the rainfall. Grass and crops need a certain amount of water in order to stay healthy and measuring the rain helps people know if there is enough to keep grass and crops in good health.

Literature

Rain Drop Splash
by Alvin Tresselt

119

Manufacturing Snowflakes

Equipment
- 6 tablespoons salt
- 6 tablespoons water
- 1 tablespoon household ammonia
- bowl
- plastic meat tray with sides • spray bottle
  (do not use metal or foil)
- 6 tablespoons bluing

Procedure
An adult needs to help with this activity. Do not eat this mixture. Make a scene in the meat tray using small rocks, tiny branches and pinecones, plastic animals and trees, or whatever you want. Carefully Glue the items to the base if necessary. Spoon mix the salt, bluing, water and ammonia in the bowl. Spray the scene lightly with water. Gently set the scene over the objects in the scene. where you can see it. Check on the scene in about two hours. What do you see? Check again every hour. How long do you think the snowflakes will grow? Do you think they are strong or fragile?

Results
The snowflakes will begin to grow in about two hours and continue to grow for several days.

Why?
The chemical action of the combined substances causes the snowflakes to grow.

Literature
The Snowy Day
by Ezra Jack Keats

Hole In A Bottle

Equipment
- plasticine clay
- pitcher
- funnel that fits the bottle opening
- 2 liter, clear plastic soft drink bottle
- water
- knife or scissors (an adult will use this)

Procedure

Put the funnel in the top of the bottle and fill the bottle with the pitcher. Is it hard? Empty the bottle. Put clay around the funnel to seal it to the neck of the bottle. Now try filling it again. Is there a difference? Next have an adult use the knife or scissors to put a small hole in the bottle near the main opening. Now try to fill the bottle. What happens? Cover the hole with your finger and try to fill the bottle. Can you do it? Take your finger off the hole and try to fill the bottle. Can you do it now?

Results

When you put the clay around the neck of the bottle, the water started to fill it up and then stopped. When you put the little hole in the bottle, the water filled it right up as long as your finger was not covering the hole.

Why?

In order for bottles to fill with water, they need to let air leave as the water goes in. If the air can't escape, it takes up space in the bottle and won't let the water in.

Literature

Amazing Air
by Henry Smith

121

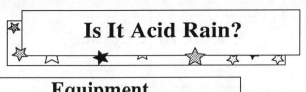
Is It Acid Rain?

Equipment
- 5 tablespoons of red cabbage juice
- 5 small glasses • rainwater
- cooled boiled water • clean jar
- lemon juice • milk
- apple juice

Procedure
Collect some rainwater in the clean jar. Put a tablespoon of red cabbage juice in each cup. Now put rainwater in one, an equal amount of cooled boiled water in the second, milk in the third, apple juice in the next, then lemon juice in the last. Label them with their contents as you fill them. What is happening in the cups? How do you know if you have acid rain? Compare the color of the cup with the rainwater with the others.

Results
Find the cup that comes closest in color to the rainwater. You can refer to a pH chart which you can find in an encyclopedia. If your mixture changes color only a little, your rainwater is normal. If it becomes as pink as the lemon solution, it has a very high acid content.

Why?
Rain is usually a little acidic because of the oxides in the air. Unpolluted rainwater measures about 5.6 on the pH scale. If your rain has a lower pH it is polluted with acid..

Literature
Michael Bird Boy
by Tomie dePaola

It's Leaking!

Equipment

- knife or scissors
- lid for the soft drink container
- water
- tape
- 2 liter, clear plastic soft drink bottle

Procedure

Do this activity outside or over a sink or tub. Fill the bottle with water and put on the lid. Have an adult make a small hole in the bottom of the bottle. Watch carefully. What happens? Gently shake the container. Does anything happen? Where is the water? Take the lid off of the container then put it back on. What happens to the hole and the leak? Now have an adult make a little hole near the top of the container. Put your finger over the hole, then take it off. What's happening? Why?

Results

No water comes out of the bottle when the lid is on. When you take the lid off, the bottle leaks. When your finger is over the hole at the top of the bottle, no water comes out, but when you take your finger off, the bottle leaks again.

Why?

When the bottle is closed, water doesn't drain out the bottom because air can't get in. As soon as the air has a way to get in the bottle through the hole in the top, the water goes out the bottom.

Literature

Muddigush
by Kimberly Knudson

123

Oxidation

Equipment
- 2 twist ties
- 2 pennies
- fingernail file
- plastic wrap
- paper towel
- rubber band
- vinegar
- salt
- bowl

Procedure

Fold a paper towel and put it in a shallow bowl. Dampen it with water, sprinkle it with a little salt and add a dash of vinegar. With the fingernail file, clean the edges of the pennies. Take the paper off the twist ties. Wrap one of the wires around a penny. Twist the other wire up into small loops. Put the pennies and the wire on the paper towel. Cover the bowl with plastic wrap. Check the bowl every few hours. What is happening? Which one is oxidizing the fastest?

Results

The twist tie wires oxidize fastest and become rusty. The pennies take longer to oxidize.

Why?

The chemical reaction of the vinegar and salt cause the rust on the twist ties and the green oxidation on the copper pennies. Based on this experiment, why do you think the Statue of Liberty looks the way it does?

Literature
And Still
The Turtle Watched
by Sheila Calahan MacGill

Slippery Solution

Equipment

- cornstarch
- small rubber ball
- water • bowl
- marble

Procedure

Mix one cup cornstarch and 3/4 cup water. This mixture should be very thick. If it is too runny, add more cornstarch. What do you think this stuff feels like? Can you pick it up? Why is it like this? Drop a small ball into the bowl. What happens to the ball? What happens to the mixture? Now drop a marble into the mixture. How does it compare to the ball?

Results

You can pick up a handful of this mixture but as soon as you do it seems to melt in your hands. When you drop the ball it stays on top of the mixture for a while and then begins to sink.

Why?

Cornstarch and water combine to make a mixture called a colloidal suspension. This means the fragments of cornstarch get evenly distributed throughout the water. When you drop the ball, the force of it falling happens too fast for the mixture to move out of the way. The mixture moves in slow motion, and the ball eventually sinks.

Literature

The Quicksand Book
by Tomie dePaola

125

PULLING IT TOGETHER

The main purpose of this book is to give children active, engaging language experiences to stimulate thinking. Emphasis is on encouraging children to be independent learners and reflective thinkers. Language tasks include guidelines for communicating about:

Observing: discriminating and noting details

Identifying: recognizing and naming objects, events, and people

Describing: discriminating important characteristics using appropriate language

Classifying: comparing, arranging, ordering, sequencing looking for relationships

Interpreting Information: cause and effect relationships comparing and contrasting

Communication: vocabulary, knowledge, asking questions, arranging ideas

Formulating Conclusions: evaluating, analyzing, organizing, summarizing

Strategies presented give children confidence to be open minded and imaginative, to differentiate facts from inference and opinions, to make organized associations, to be flexible, persistent and assured, and to make decisions and solve problems.

As a parent, grandparent and teacher, you have extraordinary impact on the learning of children. This is a book for more than reading, it is to be used. Enjoy!

BIBLIOGRAPHY

Aardema, Verna. *Bringing the Rain to Kapiti Plain,* Dial Books, 1981.

Adoff, Arnold. *Outside Inside Poems.* Lothrop, 1981.

Allen, Pamela. *Who Sank The Boat.* Coward-McCann, Inc. 1982.

Asimov, Isaac. *Air Pollution.* Gareth Stevens, Inc. 1992.

Balestrino, Philip. *Hot As An Ice Cube.* Crowell, 1971.

Bang, Molly. *The Paper Crane.* Greenwillow, 1985.

Barkin, Joanne. *Water Water Everywhere.* Silver Press, 1990.

Berenstain, Stan, and Jan Berenstain. *Science Fair.* Random House, 1977.

———. *The Trouble With Money.* Random House, 1983.

Berger, Melvin. *As Old As The Hills.* Watts, 1989.

Bishop, Pamela R. *Exploring Your Skeleton: Funny Bones and Not So Funny Bones.* Watts, 1991.

Bracy, Norma. *Salt.* Book Binder, 1986.

Branley, Franklyn M. *Air Is All Around You.* Harper and Row, 1986.

Brown, Margaret Wise. *The Important Book.* Harper and Row, 1949.

Browne, Anthony. *Changes.* Knopf Books, 1991.

Calhoun, Mary. *Hot Air Henry.* Mulberry Books, 1981.

Carlstom, Nancy. *What Does The Rain Play?* Macmillan, 1993.

Carrick, Carol. *The Highest Balloon* On The Common. Greenwillow Books, 1977.

Coerr, Eleanor. *The Big Balloon Race.* Harper and Row, 1981.

Cole, Joanna. *The Magic Schoolbus At the Waterworks.* Scholastic, 1986.

Couture, Susan Aikin. *The Block Book.* Harper, 1990.

De Paola, Tomie. *Michael Bird Boy.* Prentice-Hall, 1975.

_____. *The Popcorn Book.* Holiday, 1978.

_____. *The Quicksand Book.* Holiday, 1977.

Dorros, Arthur. *Follow The Water From Brook To Ocean.* Harper and Row, 1991.

Eastman, Patricia. *Sometimes Things Change.* Children's Press, 1983

Ets, Marie Hall. *Gilberto And The Wind.* Puffin Books, 1978.

Fowler, Allan. *It Could Still Be Water.* Children's Press, 1993.

Freeman, Don. *A Rainbow Of My Own.* Puffin Books, 1978.

Gibbons, Gail. *Boat Book.* Holiday, 1983.

Glennon, Karen. *Miss Eva and The Red Balloon.* S and S Trade, 1990.

Glimmerveen, Ulco. *A Tale Of Antartica.* Scholastic, 1989.

Glover, David. *Flying and Floating*. Kingfisher Books, 1993.

Goffin, Josse. *OH!* Harry Abrams, 1991.

Gray, Nigel. *A Balloon For Grandad*. Watts, 1988.

Healy, Jane M. PhD. *Is Your Bed Still There When You Close The Door?* Doubleday, 1992.

Hendersen, Kathy. *Where Does It Come From? Water*. MacDonald, 1986.

Hoban, Lillian. *The Sugar Snow Spring*. Harper, 1973.

Hoban, Tana. *Look Again*. Macmillan, 1971.

Hohmann, Mary. Bernard Banet and Davie P. Weikart. Young *Children In Action*. High Scope Press, 1979.

Holl, Adelaide. *The Rain Puddle*. Lothrop, 1965.

Joly, Dominique. *Grains of Salt*. Young Discovery Library, 1988.

Jonas, Ann. *Round Trip*. Greenwillow, 1983.

Keats, Ezra Jack. *The Snowy Day*. Puffin Books, 1976.

Kipling, Rudyard. *How The Camel Got His Hump*. Crown, 1978.

Kirkpatrick, Rena K. *Look At Magnets*. Steck Vaughn, 1985.

Knutson, Kimberly, *Muddigush*. Macmillan, 1992.

Konigsburg, E. L. *Samuel Todd's Book of Great Colors*. Macmillan, 1990.

Lamorisse, Albert. *The Red Balloon*. Doubleday, 1956.

Leedy, Loreen. *Messages In The Mailbox*. Holiday, 1991.

Lenssen, Ann. *A Rainbow Balloon*. Cobblehill Books, 1992.

Lionni, Leo. *Little Blue, Little Yellow*. Astor, 1959.

Loretan, Sylvia. *Bob The Snowman*. Viking Penguin, 1988.

MacGill, Calahan Shiela. *And Still The Turtle Watched*. Dial, 1991.

Markle, Sandra. *A Rainy Day*. Watts, 1993.

Michel, Francois. *Water*. Lothrop, 1993.

Morgan, Allen. *Sadie and The Snowman*. Scholastic, 1985.

Nicklaus, Carol. *Eggs-O-Poppin*. Random Books. 1993.

O'Neal, Debbie. and Amelia Rosato. *The Lost Coin*. Judson, 1993.

Palmer, Joy. *Snow and Ice*. Big Song Book, 1993.

Parks, Barbara. *Skinny Bones*. Knopf Books, 1989.

Primavera, Elise. *Ralph's Frozen Tale*. Putnam, 1991.

Robbins, Ken. *Make Me A Peanut Butter Sandiwch and a Glass of Milk*. Scholastic, 1992.

Schenk de Regniers, Beatrice. *Sing A Song Of Popcorn*. Scholastic, 1988.

Shulevitz, Uri. *Rain Rain Rivers*. Farrar, 1969.

Simon, Seymour. *Icebergs and Glaciers*. Morrow, 1987.

Sis, Peter. *Rainbow Rhino*. Knopf Books, 1987.

Smith, Jerry. *Up Goes Mr. Downs*. Parents, 1985.

Smith, Henry. *Amazing Air*. Morrow, 1983.

Stanley, Diane. *The Good Luck Pencil.* Macmillan, 1986.

Thaler, Mike. In *The Middle of The Puddle.* Harper and Row, 1988.

Tresselt, Alvin. *Rain Drop Splash.* Morrow, 1990.

Tzannes, Robin. and Paul Korky. *Professor Puffendorf's Secret Potions.* Checkerboard, 1992.

Viorst, Judith. *Alexander Who Used To Be Rich Last Sunday.* Macmillan, 1978.

Wallner, John. *Hailstones and Halibut Bones.* Doubleday, 1989.

Walsh, Ellen Stoll. *Mouse Paint.* Harcourt Brace, 1989.

Weisner, David. *June 29, 1999.* Clarion Books, 1992.

Wildsmith, Brian. *Bears Adventure.* Pantheon, 1982.

Wyler, Rose. *Raindrops and Rainbows.* Messner, 1989.

Yolen, Jane. *Letting Swift River Go.* Little Brown and Co., 1992.

Yolen, Jane. *The Girl Who Loved The Wind.* Thomas Crowell, 1972.